The Computer Lab Teacher's Survival Guide

Second Edition

K–6 Units for the Whole Year

Holly Poteete

International Society for Technology in Education
EUGENE, OREGON • WASHINGTON, DC

The Computer Lab Teacher's Survival Guide
K–6 Units for the Whole Year
Second Edition

Holly Poteete

© 2010 International Society for Technology in Education

Director of Book Publishing: *Courtney Burkholder*
Acquisitions Editor: *Jeff V. Bolkan*
Production Editor: *Lanier Brandau, Lynda Gansel*
Production Coordinator: *Rachel Bannister*
Graphic Designer: *Signe Landin*
Copy Editor: *Kathy Hamman*
Cover and Book Design: *Kim McGovern*

Library of Congress Cataloging-in-Publication Data

Poteete, Holly.
    The computer lab teacher's survival guide: k/6 units for the whole year /
    Holly Poteete. — 2nd ed.
      p. cm.
    ISBN 978-1-56484-260-2 (pbk.)
      1. Educational technology. 2. Computer-assisted instruction.   I. Title.
    LB1028.43.P673 2009
    372.133'4—dc22

                                                                   2009037645

Second Edition
ISBN: 978-1-56484-262-6

Printed in the United States of America

International Society for Technology in Education (ISTE)
Washington, DC, Office:
    1710 Rhode Island Ave. NW, Suite 900, Washington, DC 20036-3132
Eugene, Oregon, Office:
    180 West 8th Ave., Suite 300, Eugene, OR 97401-2916
Order Desk: 1.800.336.5191
Order Fax: 1.541.302.3778
Customer Service: orders@iste.org
Book Publishing: books@iste.org
Rights and Permissions: permissions@iste.org
Book Sales and Marketing: booksmarketing@iste.org
Web: www.iste.org

Photos: ©iStockphoto.com
Unit 1, Catherine Yeulet; Unit 3, Marilyn Nieves; Unit 5, Daaron J.;
Units 6 and 9. Lisa F. Young; Units 7 and 10, Morgan Lane; Unit 8, Répási Lajos.

About ISTE

The International Society for Technology in Education (ISTE) is the trusted source for professional development, knowledge generation, advocacy, and leadership for innovation. A nonprofit membership association, ISTE provides leadership and service to improve teaching, learning, and school leadership by advancing the effective use of technology in PK–12 and teacher education.

Home of the National Educational Technology Standards (NETS), the Center for Applied Research in Educational Technology (CARET), and ISTE's annual conference and exposition (formerly known as the National Educational Computing Conference, or NECC), ISTE represents more than 100,000 professionals worldwide. We support our members with information, networking opportunities, and guidance as they face the challenge of transforming education. To find out more about these and other ISTE initiatives, visit our website at **www.iste.org**.

As part of our mission, ISTE Book Publishing works with experienced educators to develop and produce practical resources for classroom teachers, teacher educators, and technology leaders. Every manuscript we select for publication is carefully peer-reviewed and professionally edited. We value your feedback on this book and other ISTE products. E-mail us at **books@iste.org**.

About the Author

Holly Poteete draws on more than 11 years of experience with elementary and middle schools across the country. In addition to her classroom experience, she has taught technology classes for educators and parents. The Georgia Department of Education has published many of her web-based lesson plans that integrate technology with core curriculum standards. Holly is the author of *Kids, Computers, and Learning: An Activity Guide for Parents,* an ISTE's HomePage book imprint. She believes in the importance of instilling the desire to master skills in students.

Holly and her husband, Paul, are the parents of two children and reside in Monterey, California.

Contents

Introduction 1

    Organization of This Book 2

    NETS•S Addressed in the Lessons...4

    How Can I Successfully Teach Technology? 5

    The Computer Lab 7

UNIT 1

Welcome and Pretest 13

UNIT 2

The Internet..21

    LESSON 1 • How the Internet Works...24

    LESSON 2 • The World Wide Web..31

UNIT 3

Keyboarding 39

    LESSON 1 • Keyboarding Technique 42

    LESSON 2 • Keyboarding Practice 51

    LESSON 3 • Keyboarding Assessment 59

UNIT 4

Digital Citizenship 69

    LESSON 1 • Responsible Use of Technology 72

    LESSON 2 • Internet Safety and Netiquette.................................79

UNIT 5

Peripheral Devices 85

    LESSON 1 • Peripheral Devices Basics...88

    LESSON 2 • Peripheral Devices Identification..............................95

UNIT 6

Internet Research and Creativity 103

LESSON 1 • Internet Research 106

LESSON 2 • Slide Creation 113

LESSON 3 • Research Presentations... 120

UNIT 7

Internet Messaging and Communications........................... 127

LESSON 1 • Electronic Mail 130

LESSON 2 • Instant Messaging 139

LESSON 3 • VoIP and Videoconferencing...................................... 147

UNIT 8

Multimedia Presentations 155

LESSON 1 • Storyboarding.. 157

LESSON 2 • Multimedia Slide Shows 163

LESSON 3 • Slide Show Presentations... 170

UNIT 9

Online Learning 177

LESSON 1 • Virtual Field Trips 180

LESSON 2 • Online Encyclopedias 187

UNIT 10

Web 2.0 195

LESSON 1 • Blogs.. 198

LESSON 2 • Podcasts 206

Appendix

National Educational Technology Standards for Teachers (NETS•T) 215

Introduction

Since the 1994 National Educational Technology Goals 2000: Educate America Act, technology has poured into our school systems. Often this technology is concentrated in a computer lab. The purpose of *The Computer Lab Teacher's Survival Guide, Second Edition* is to provide a framework for schools to ensure that all students are receiving an appropriate, effective, and up-to-date technology education. This book offers a complete curriculum that integrates instruction on technology with computer activities.

Teachers and administrators are constantly looking for ways to simplify yet broaden the scope of technology in the classroom. While many books are designed to help teachers integrate technology into the curriculum, few of these books are specifically directed at computer lab instructors, who are in immediate need of creative ways to teach students technology use. Throughout my 11 years of experience in working with students in various schools throughout the United States, I have discovered some interesting ideas and have developed approaches to technology instruction in the computer lab setting. This book offers ideas and a curriculum for the computer lab teacher.

The supplements included on the accompanying compact disc may be used with *The Computer Lab Teacher's Survival Guide* curriculum. On the CD are more than 100 supplemental files, including multimedia presentations (provided as PowerPoint files), worksheets, quizzes, addresses for websites, and other documents used in the lessons (provided as both Word documents and PDF files). Teachers may wish to create a supplemental notebook by printing all of the CD files and placing them in a three-ring binder, making the documents easy to copy and distribute for each class.

The lessons in this book are a guide for your own ideas and concepts. You can create an individual vision and theme for your computer lab to motivate and inspire the students in your care. The lessons in this book are only a starting point. Tap into your own teaching style to enrich the units I have provided. Even more important than the curriculum in this book is the hidden curriculum, the way the teacher portrays the lessons to the students. With the ideas in these lessons and your own personal flair, you can empower students with technological information.

Students will see your excitement and catch the flame. Students will experience technology in your lab or classroom more enthusiastically as they engage in new and inspiring activities. Understanding technology has become a necessity in today's society, and students with a solid background in technology will have the foundation necessary to succeed in the future. Often schools cannot afford or acquire specifically trained technology instructors; this book gives educators of diverse training backgrounds the tools they need to teach technology effectively.

The activities in this book will motivate, inspire, and promote technology-driven lessons in the computer lab. When students are told to play games and complete unsupervised activities, the computer lab has lost its usefulness. This book is a complete curriculum that integrates instruction on technology with computer activities. Students are motivated and inspired to become proficient in the use of technology while learning technological concepts. Employ the more than 100 supplements on the accompanying CD to enrich and support the lessons.

Organization of This Book

The main section of this book is divided into 10 curriculum units. Each unit (except Unit 1, a shorter preliminary section) includes two or three lessons that expand on the unit concepts. The National Educational Technology Standards for Students (NETS•S) can be found on pages 4–5. The National Educational Technology Standards for Teachers (NETS•T) are in the Appendix after the curriculum units. The following paragraphs discuss the content and arrangement of the units and lessons in greater detail.

Unit Format

Each unit (with the exception of Unit 1) has an introduction that provides an overview of the lessons, a unit goal, ideas about accommodating younger students, and suggestions for room decorations. Also, a section identifies the NETS•S addressed.

Lesson Format

Each lesson includes sections identifying the objective, materials and equipment needed, associated CD files (called Supplements), and procedures, as well as ideas for younger students, lesson extensions, remediation, and accommodation.

This book is a complete curriculum with more than 100 files on the accompanying CD, including worksheets, slide show presentations, activities, and lists of websites. Lists of examples are provided throughout the lessons to offer instructional suggestions. Some of these examples are included on the CD.

The lessons include the following components:

Objective

This section provides an overview for guiding the students through the lesson and describes the expectations for students by the end of the lesson.

Materials and Equipment

A detailed list of the items and any special equipment needed to teach the lesson is presented in this section. Optional materials are included.

Supplement List

This section itemizes all the associated files for the lesson provided on the accompanying CD.

Procedures

The Procedures section provides the steps for teaching the lesson. The information is presented in the following categories:

> **Motivation.** The Motivation discussion offers activities to focus the students' attention on the upcoming lesson. It may suggest a fun event, short practice, or skill development exercise.

Purpose. Use the information in the Purpose category to inform students about the skills or knowledge they will have by the end of the lesson and to describe why the lesson is important.

Instructional Input. This section discusses the meat of the lesson. You will present this information to students using a multimedia presentation, document, online game, or activity.

Check for Understanding. This section offers ideas for checking student comprehension, such as posing questions or asking for feedback.

Guided Practice. This category offers ideas for having students practice the lesson objective while monitored and guided by the teacher.

Independent Practice. This section provides guidance for having students practice the lesson objective independently inside or outside the classroom.

Assessment. The Assessment category discusses methods for evaluating student comprehension, including observation, tests, worksheets, and out-of-class assignments.

Closure. This section sums up the lesson in a few words and offers concluding remarks and simple activities.

Extension

The Extension section provides examples of activities for students who finish early or who need a more challenging learning activity.

Remediation

The Remediation discussion provides extra practice or simplified activities for students who need extra help with the lesson.

Accommodation

This section provides assistance ideas for students with special needs.

NETS•S Addressed in the Lessons

Each lesson is designed to address one or more of the newly revised National Educational Technology Standards for Students (NETS•S), 2007. The specific standards addressed are listed in the preliminary discussion for each unit. The complete NETS•S are presented here, and the new National Educational Technology Standards for Teachers can be found in the Appendix.

National Educational Technology Standards for Students (NETS•S)

1. **Creativity and Innovation**

   Students demonstrate creative thinking, construct knowledge, and develop innovative products and processes using technology. Students:

   a. apply existing knowledge to generate new ideas, products, or processes

   b. create original works as a means of personal or group expression

   c. use models and simulations to explore complex systems and issues

   d. identify trends and forecast possibilities

2. **Communication and Collaboration**

   Students use digital media and environments to communicate and work collaboratively, including at a distance, to support individual learning and contribute to the learning of others. Students:

   a. interact, collaborate, and publish with peers, experts, or others employing a variety of digital environments and media

   b. communicate information and ideas effectively to multiple audiences using a variety of media and formats

   c. develop cultural understanding and global awareness by engaging with learners of other cultures

   d. contribute to project teams to produce original works or solve problems

3. **Research and Information Fluency**

   Students apply digital tools to gather, evaluate, and use information. Students:

   a. plan strategies to guide inquiry

   b. locate, organize, analyze, evaluate, synthesize, and ethically use information from a variety of sources and media

   c. evaluate and select information sources and digital tools based on the appropriateness to specific tasks

   d. process data and report results

4. **Critical Thinking, Problem Solving, and Decision Making**

   Students use critical thinking skills to plan and conduct research, manage projects, solve problems, and make informed decisions using appropriate digital tools and resources. Students:

   a. identify and define authentic problems and significant questions for investigation

   b. plan and manage activities to develop a solution or complete a project

   c. collect and analyze data to identify solutions and/or make informed decisions

   d. use multiple processes and diverse perspectives to explore alternative solutions

5. **Digital Citizenship**

   Students understand human, cultural, and societal issues related to technology and practice legal and ethical behavior. Students:

   a. advocate and practice safe, legal, and responsible use of information and technology

   b. exhibit a positive attitude toward using technology that supports collaboration, learning, and productivity

   c. demonstrate personal responsibility for lifelong learning

   d. exhibit leadership for digital citizenship

6. **Technology Operations and Concepts**

   Students demonstrate a sound understanding of technology concepts, systems, and operations. Students:

   a. understand and use technology systems

   b. select and use applications effectively and productively

   c. troubleshoot systems and applications

   d. transfer current knowledge to learning of new technologies

How Can I Successfully Teach Technology?

The best way to successfully teach technology is to be yourself. Cultivate a positive learning environment that inspires students to reach beyond ordinary methods of learning. Students will be motivated by your enthusiastic attitude toward technology and willingness to learn new concepts. This curriculum is easy to follow and modify for a variety of instructional methods and styles. As always, it is important to plan as much as possible; however, be willing to adapt the lesson in the classroom using new strategies. As technological innovations occur, many traditional classrooms will be transformed. Soon every teacher will need a thorough understanding of incorporating technology into the classroom to provide a proper education.

Technology has changed the way we live and will continue to revolutionize our world. Students easily adapt to innovations in technology and revolutionary ideas in education. Because students have no fear when deciphering a computer issue or solving a technical problem, a variety of new activities can and should be incorporated into lessons to teach technological concepts. These activities could include:

- Collaborative online work
- Multimedia presentations
- Telecommunications
- Real-world uses of technology
- Online information exchange
- Student-centered learning
- Discovery learning
- Internet research

You are creating a technological foundation for students every day that they are in your care. Remember to use as your guide the NETS•S, which provide specific outcomes for students' abilities in technology. The techniques of instructing students using technology are endless, just as the methods of traditional instruction are unlimited. Envision a classroom environment that will best meet the needs of your students. Your excitement and new ideas will inspire the students to become highly technologically literate lifelong learners.

Technical Difficulties

I have experienced many technical difficulties while teaching technology, but technical difficulties can be learning experiences, too. For example, at the beginning of one year, the fuse blew for half of the computers in the lab. I decided to use this as a learning tool about electricity and technology. I began questioning the students in an organized and struc-tured way, which allowed me to include the entire class in the discussion. The students determined that the power was off for many of the computers. I asked the students, "What should we do?" The students responded with several suggestions. One student said we should make sure the network cables were plugged in. I responded with the question, "Does the network cable provide power to the computers?" Several students responded until one student came to the realization that power had been lost.

I asked the students again, "What should we do?" The students said we needed to get power back to the computers and that we should call the maintenance office to let them know about the problem. I called the maintenance office, using the speakerphone to involve the students in every step of solving the difficulty. After I had made the call and began discussing alternative activities with the class, I saw several students talking quietly among themselves. When I requested their attention, they asked if I had planned the fuse to blow just to teach them a lesson in troubleshooting computers.

After that question, I realized that the entire event had become an exciting learning adven-ture. The students had learned the concept of troubleshooting through my questions about the technical problem, and they probably learned more that day about troubleshooting and thinking on their toes than the planned computer activity could have taught them.

The Computer Lab

Teaching in a computer lab is different from teaching in a regular classroom. In some schools, teachers are expected to take their class to the computer lab during exploratory or teacher planning periods and have the students work independently on the computers. It is common practice for teachers to sit in the classroom, allowing the students to "play" games on the computer with very little monitoring or instruction. Similarly, some schools require paraprofessionals to monitor the students as they "play" on the computers. However, learning technology is just like any other type of learning. Students need an organized structure for learning technology to compete in this age of information.

When I began teaching technology, I realized the ease with which students understood the concepts. I created an intense atmosphere for learning in the lab. All of my students had used a computer before, and most had a computer at home. Rather than letting them play games, I decided to bring the students to a new level of expertise. I used the NETS•S as a foundation to instruct my classes, and the students' technological skills and awareness grew tremendously. The following ideas may help you make your computer lab more welcoming and efficient.

Every three years technology becomes outdated and usually needs to be replaced. Since technology changes so fast, the way we use computer labs may change as well. Schools may decide to use technology inside the classroom instead of going to a computer lab to use technology. Many schools already have laptops and computer projectors that you can reserve to be used in the class while teaching a particular lesson. The concepts and ideas given in this book for a computer lab can also be used in the classroom.

Atmosphere

Atmosphere is an integral part of a successful computer laboratory. When the students walk into the lab, they should see and feel a structured technology classroom. Create a positive and engaging atmosphere by integrating the lesson structure and classroom design, which should display technology in a fun, colorful, and organized fashion.

Appearances matter. The room should be vacuumed regularly, and trash should be kept off the floor. Also, the tables, monitors, and towers should be dusted and cleaned frequently. If the school shows respect for computers, so will the students. The computer wires and cables in the lab should be out of sight. There are many ways to cover and hide the cables, for example, specially made tables, drop boxes, corrugated tubing, cable ties, Velcro ties, or self-adhesive cord holders, just to name a few.

Decide on a fun theme for the computer lab, such as fish, frogs, rain forests, the ocean, farm animals, or anything else of interest. Label the computers with numbers using the theme. For example, if the theme is frogs, tape a small, brightly colored frog to the front, top left of each monitor displaying the computer number. Go to a fabric or discount store to buy cheerful colored fabric displaying the theme and cut it out to create the background for one of the bulletin boards. The fabric may also be used as a tablecloth for the printer table or other surface. Decorate the room with several objects hanging from the ceiling related to the theme. You could even place a lively theme carpet in a special location in the room.

The room should have several bulletin boards decorated with brightly colored paper and computer borders. School supply stores offer a variety of computer-related borders and posters. Go online and search for decorations for use in your classroom.

Computer Lab Management

One computer lab management technique is to place a plastic cup next to each monitor. (Tape a picture or cutout of your theme onto the cup for fun.) When a student has a question, he or she places the cup on top of the monitor to alert the teacher but keeps working if the teacher is helping another student. When using this method, you may find that by the time you get the opportunity to help, the student has been able to figure out the answer on his or her own.

Come up with a standard method of getting the students' attention quickly. This signal could be clapping in a special rhythm, ringing a bell, raising your hand, or anything else that quickly and easily gets the students to focus on you.

Keep a box at the front of the classroom filled with small prizes. At the end of class choose the quietest, the best behaved, or the most active participant to come up to the box and choose a prize. Remember to mark which students have received a prize so that all students in the class have an opportunity to come to the prize box during the year.

It is important to make a seating chart for each class so that the students know exactly where to sit when they arrive. A seating chart will also help you to remember the students' names quickly.

Remember to promote student participation and support students by encouraging them to do their best. It is important to have a lot of patience with the students in the computer lab.

Keep a class set of pencils and some paper readily available because many of the lessons require some writing. Also, you will be prepared in case of an unforeseen computer problem; you can assign a writing or drawing activity while working on the computer situation.

The computers should be set up in rows facing the classroom screen used for projected images, with a large aisle down the center of the room. This allows all students to see the screen and lets you view all monitors to see whether students are on task. This setup provides the best instructional and the least restrictive environment.

Following these guidelines when designing a computer lab will create a fun atmosphere for learning technology, and the students will sense a positive structure in the room and the curriculum.

Ergonomics for Students

A growing number of students are using computers at home and at school for long periods of time. With the increased use of computers comes a higher risk of injury, including neck pain, back pain, and carpal tunnel syndrome. Designing safe and healthy computing environments as well as developing correct posture strategies will educate students on this important issue.

Think about the best solution for your classroom to promote health and wellness among students in your care. The specific hardware devices and the arrangement of the computer lab should be carefully studied to determine whether any changes should be made to meet the needs of the students more effectively. If your school has little or no budget for this, there are some inexpensive plans you can implement to make the computer lab safer.

Teach students at an early age the correct way to sit at the keyboard and the proper arrangement of the workstation to meet their comfort level. It is also important to teach students the reason for sitting with the correct posture and ensuring the workstation meets their individual needs. If students understand that developing bad habits may cause them injuries that will prevent them from playing sports or using the computer for a while, they will probably listen and try to follow the guidelines you set in the classroom. Talk to the students about how it would make them feel if they were unable to play baseball or use their computers for six months. Try to get the students to understand the importance of correct posture and the proper arrangement of the computer workstation.

The following lists provide guidelines and suggestions for ensuring the safe use of computers in your lab. Instruct students to be aware of the position of their body when using the computer, and arrange the room to meet the needs of the students.

Monitor

- Dim the lights, and close the blinds or curtains to minimize the glare on monitors so that students do not have to strain to see the computer screen. If the lights are dimmed, make sure the students can read any documents without straining their eyes.

- Arrange the computers so that the monitors do not face the windows.

- Depending upon the size of the monitor, arrange the monitor so that it is far enough away from the student. The text or upper portion of the screen should be at eye level so students are not straining their necks to see the screen. The monitor can be slightly adjusted up and down for different heights.

- Use lamps or free-standing miniature lights at each computer station if students need to read or write while using the computer.

Keyboard and Mouse

- Buy wrists pads or make your own by rolling up a small cloth.

- Acquire small keyboards and mice for younger students. Students with small hands will be better able to reach the keys on a smaller keyboard and to move a smaller mouse.

- Ensure that the mouse is easily reachable. If the students are not using the keyboard, it could be moved to the side and the mouse moved to the center so that the mouse is closer to them while working.

- If keyboard legs are available, adjust them so that the students are most comfortable when typing.

- Ensure that the students' arms are straight and parallel to the keyboard, and elbows are by their sides. If a taller chair is not available, the students could sit on a chair pad or foam so their arms are in the correct position.

- Make sure that students are using the proper keyboarding position. The correct position is discussed in Unit 3, Keyboarding. Here are some things to remember:

    - Eyes on monitor
    - Wrists flat
    - Fingers curved
    - Feet flat on floor
    - Back straight
    - Fingers on home row

- Ensure that students are sitting comfortably in the correct keyboarding position. While students are working, their shoulders should be relaxed.

- Have students use a document holder so that they do not have to strain their necks when looking at documents.

Chair

- Have students sit with their backs straight. If the chairs are curved or bent, a back-pillow or foam could be used inside the back of the chair so that students' backs are supported against the chair backs while they are typing.

- Direct students to sit with their feet on the floor. If a student's feet do not reach the floor, a footstool, backpack, or old phone books can be used as footrests.

- Ensure that students can easily view text on the screen without bending their necks up. Students can sit on foam pads so their eyes can focus on the middle and top portions of the monitor.

Breaks

- While they are working, encourage students to stretch or take a break. The class can do a few stretches together, or students may walk around and look at other students' work when appropriate.

- Teach simple exercises, such as raising arms, opening and closing hands, touching toes, and reaching for the sky. Complete these when the students are sitting at the computer and working for long periods of time. You can make up a song to help students remember to stretch when using the computer.

If students understand the importance of sitting correctly and arranging the workstation appropriately at school, they will be more aware of these concerns when using the computer at home. Your school could hold a workshop to teach parents about the importance of healthy computing in the home. A checklist worksheet could be provided for parents to assess their home computer workstation to determine whether any modifications need to be made for their children.

Internet Security

From anti-virus to encryption, there are many ways to secure the information on the computers in the computer lab. Students should be able to be creative and explore technology in a safe digital environment. Teachers need to be aware of the delicate balance: allowing students to use technology and the Internet while protecting them from the dangers that go along with online learning. Because each computer lab has different equipment and technologies, here are a few general ideas and simple steps to consider when determining if your computer lab or portable computer lab is secure.

Step 1. Determine the current security state in your computer lab.

- Perform a quick assessment of your computers or servers.
- Consider the time it would take for a hacker to access private information.
- Think about any vulnerable areas that could be compromised.

Step 2. What level of security do you want for the computer lab?

- Secure private information on the school's server.
- Use encryption for certain drives to protect sensitive information in the event the drive or system is lost or stolen.
- Protect computers from viruses and malicious hacker attacks.

Step 3. How are you going to achieve your goal?

- Create a technology security plan.
- Use web-filtering software or an appliance when allowing students to access the Internet.
- Install a firewall plus anti-virus and anti-spyware software.
- Create student logins and passwords.
- Encrypt the drives of laptops that contain sensitive information and access the school network.

There are many ways to secure your network, so work with your network administrator to determine the best options for the computer lab to protect the information and the students most effectively.

Welcome
and Pretest

Unit Overview

Wow, this is the first lesson of the year! Be creative, and enjoy yourself with this experience in technology education. Let the students know that this year will be a fun learning adventure! Your enthusiasm for teaching technology will excite the students in a whole new way.

Objective

Using a variety of methods, introduce students to the computer lab, explain the school policies relating to technology and the computer lab, and assess students to determine their current technology competencies.

Materials and Equipment

- paper and pencil for each student
- dry erase board and markers or chalkboard and chalk
- index cards (optional)
- computer projection device
- Supplements 1A, 1B, 1C, 1D, 1E, 1F, 1G, 1H, and 1I

Supplement List

Below is a list of the lesson supplements that are on the accompanying CD, which is located in the back of this book. Use the CD to open the supplements and modify them, if desired.

SUPPLEMENT	TITLE	FORMAT
1A	Welcome Slide Show	PowerPoint Presentation
1B	Computer Lab Daily Lesson Plan	Word Document
1C	Computer Lab Syllabus	Word Document
1D	Computer Lab Homework Record	Word Document
1E	Technology Pretest I	Word Document
1F	Technology Pretest II	Word Document
1G	Technology Pretest I Answers	Word Document
1H	Technology Pretest II Answers	Word Document
1I	Glossary	Word Document

Procedures

Motivation

Use this opening activity, the Welcome Slide Show (CD Supplement 1A), to inspire and energize students to learn about computers and technology. This lesson is vital for creating a positive learning environment for students and for generating momentum for the remainder of the school year. Creatively incorporate your personal teaching style to share enthusiasm and stimulate learning while providing the best activity for each grade level. The following list offers ideas for launching this lesson.

EXAMPLES

- Project the Welcome Slide Show (CD Supplement 1A) onto the classroom screen as students enter the room. The presentation offers introductory statements about the class.

- Encourage students to share their past experiences with technology. The students could take turns stating their names and telling something they know about technology or computers.

- Share your personal experiences with technology that will inspire students. They will realize that you have a personal interest in computers and that you enjoy teaching and using technology.

- Have students share personal goals or dreams about technology. This relates their lives to the computer lab course. Some students may be inspired to consider careers using technology.

- Explain and demonstrate to students new technologies in the computer lab, including software, computers, or projectors.

- Discuss the technology vision or plan for your school with the students to build excitement about the lab.

Purpose

This first class of the year provides an introduction to the computer lab and a great opportunity to ascertain students' preexisting knowledge about technology. It is also important to set up and explain classroom management procedures that will be used for the rest of the year.

Instructional Input

Computer lab policies and expectations are the heart of this discussion. Careful consideration and planning will determine the most appropriate instruction method for each grade level. For guidance and ideas, refer to the instruction samples for various grades on the Computer Lab Daily Lesson Plan (CD Supplement 1B).

Think about essential information pertaining to technology that you may need to discuss with students to prepare for the year. Be flexible. You may need to change plans depending upon the needs of students. Infuse energy into your style and actively engage students while teaching.

EXAMPLES

- Read and discuss with the class the Computer Lab Syllabus (CD Supplement 1C). The syllabus could be placed on the school's website for parents to view.

- Distribute the Computer Lab Homework Record (CD Supplement 1D). Discuss the importance of requiring parents to sign the homework sheet.

- Require students to get a folder for the computer lab in which to keep assignments, the Computer Lab Syllabus, and the Computer Lab Homework Record (CD Supplements 1C and 1D).

- Discuss special school technology projects and highlights of the upcoming year to excite the students, such as new computers added to classrooms, e-mail communication with teachers, school blogs, and the school website.

- Explain the school's Technology Code of Ethics policy and the school's Acceptable Use Policy. Throughout the school year, these topics should be repeated and discussed.

- Discuss technology initiatives that are particular to your school, such as networks, passwords, e-mail, portable media devices, teacher computers, and the use of computers before and after school.

- Explain the rules for the computer lab, including basic classroom management, so the students will be aware of all that is expected throughout the year. Discuss possible consequences if the computer lab policies are not followed.

- Explain the use of plastic cups as a classroom management technique. While working independently at computers, if a student has a question for the teacher, the student places the cup on top of the monitor or tower so the teacher is able to quickly view students needing assistance. This enables students to continue working until the instructor arrives.

Check for Understanding

Students should have a clear understanding of all that is expected of them during the school year. When asking questions, try to call on various students, encourage student collaboration, and provide positive feedback. Visual and verbal clues may reveal that the students do not fully understand the concepts and that you need to teach the lesson again in a different way.

EXAMPLES

- Allow the students to retell some of the concepts that were discussed.

- Provide students with an opportunity to ask questions, or ask the students questions.

Guided Practice

Create a fun, yet organized atmosphere that encourages students to feel self-confident as they review computer lab policies. Carefully consider which student-centered approaches will allow students to become actively involved and ponder new technological ideas. Use rewards such as small prizes, stickers, and words of encouragement to motivate students to participate in class discussions.

EXAMPLES

- Play a game based on the information discussed in this lesson.

  1. Create a list of questions based on your school's technology procedures. Write the questions on index cards, using one question per card.

  2. Have students take turns reading and answering the questions to win points for a team.

  3. After all questions have been answered, announce the team with the most points as the winner.

- Direct students to write a question concerning the computer lab on paper. Have the students take turns asking and answering questions.

Independent Practice

This independent practice involves having students demonstrate their knowledge of technology. Spend some time explaining the activity so that students will understand your expectations. Your excitement about technology will become contagious and will encourage students to do their very best. Determine the most effective technique for each grade level for discovering student knowledge. The following ideas may help.

EXAMPLES

- Give Technology Pretest I (CD Supplement 1E) to older students to determine their technology expertise. Read the questions aloud for students learning to read.

- Assign Technology Pretest II (CD Supplement 1F) to younger students to determine their technical abilities. A Scantron answer sheet can be used to correct the pretests.

- Encourage students to share "what they know" and "what they want to know" through a collaborative brainstorming activity. Write ideas on the board or type ideas using the computer projector. When students are given an opportunity to provide input, the information learned can be claimed as their own.

- Have students write down facts they know about computers or technology, as well as technology they would like to learn more about. The students could then share their thoughts and ideas.

- Implement a computer literacy assessment from the ISTE *Educator Resources* website: www.iste.org/AM/Template.cfm?Section=Assessment&Template=/TaggedPage/TaggedPageDisplay.cfm&TPLID=23&ContentID=13481.

Assessment

A variety of methods could be used to assess students on this lesson. Use the most appropriate method for each grade level and class. Give the students several ways to succeed, and adjust the evaluation to the style of instruction.

EXAMPLES

- Use the Technology Pretest I Answers and Technology Pretest II Answers (CD Supplements 1G and 1H) to correct the pretests, or have students check their own papers.

- Observe students throughout the lesson to determine comprehension and abilities.

- Assess students based on their class participation throughout the lesson. The seating chart or the class roll could be used to record student participation during class.

Closure

Students should feel confident and proud about their level of expertise concerning technology and excited about the prospect of learning new ideas and skills this year in the computer lab. Students should also understand that technology is an important part of life and that becoming proficient in technology use will help students become productive citizens. This first lesson of the first semester will have provided a foundation for the upcoming school year. Conclude it with encouragement and excitement for learning.

EXAMPLES

- As a homework task, ask older students to obtain a folder for computer lab assignments. This folder should be kept organized and brought to each computer class; periodic folder checks could be implemented. Students could write their first homework assignment on the Computer Lab Homework Record (CD Supplement 1D).

- Award a prize from the prize box located at the front of the classroom to one student in the class. Choose a different hard-working student to receive the prize for each class, so at the end of the year, everyone should have had the chance to receive a prize.

Extension

Motivated students will attempt innovative tasks. Allowing students to become involved in the learning process will make the knowledge personally meaningful. Think of creative ideas that could be incorporated in or out of the classroom to inspire students to undertake new challenges.

EXAMPLES

- Use the results from Technology Pretest I or Technology Pretest II (CD Supplements 1E and 1F), as well as class participation, to select an executive technology intern to assist in everyday maintenance of the computer lab, including cleaning monitors, booting up computers, shutting down computers, installing software, and assessing computer problems.

- Distribute the Glossary (CD Supplement 1I) to students so that they will be able to look up important terms throughout the year.

- Choose one or more technology experts per class to perform certain tasks during class, during school breaks, before school, or after school. This develops leadership skills and provides students with extra technology instruction.

- Have students think of a high-level question concerning technology and write it on paper. Collect the papers and write the answers for the students on their papers. Return the answers during the next computer lab class.

- Have students research and design a Technology Acceptable Use Policy for the computer lab at your school. Students could also design a Technology Acceptable Use Policy for their home computer(s).

Remediation

Throughout the lesson, observe students to locate any struggling with the concepts. Assist these students when noticed, or provide guidance at another time. Contemplate a way to meet the needs of students having difficulties with comprehension.

EXAMPLES

- Engage the students in active learning throughout the lesson by allowing them to interact with peers to ensure understanding.

- Use an interesting manipulative or drama when teaching to captivate students. Try other alternative instruction methods with those having difficulty.

Accommodation

Be sensitive to students with special needs or disabilities and make modifications to the lesson depending on individual needs. Consider the best ways to modify the lesson to provide the least restrictive environment for these students.

EXAMPLES

- Read the pretest aloud to the students with special needs. The pretest could be shortened to maximize success for these students.

- Allow the students with special needs extra time to complete the assessment.
- Use assistive technology devices to accommodate students with special needs in the computer lab.

UNIT 2

The Internet

Unit Overview

This unit on the Internet includes two lessons: How the Internet Works and The World Wide Web. Students will use online learning tutorials to learn about technology and process this information using a variety of methods. In the first lesson, How the Internet Works, students will learn about the basic infrastructure of the Internet using online learning tutorials and then complete a worksheet reinforcing specific terms. In the next lesson, The World Wide Web, students will learn about web browsers and the World Wide Web and then work collaboratively to complete an online scavenger hunt using the techniques learned. At the completion of the Internet unit, students should have a sound understanding of how the Internet works and how to navigate the World Wide Web.

Unit Goal

To give students an understanding of Internet infrastructure and basic navigation on the World Wide Web using online learning tutorials.

NETS•S Addressed

3. **Research and Information Fluency**

   Students apply digital tools to gather, evaluate, and use information. Students:

   a.   plan strategies to guide inquiry

   b.   locate, organize, analyze, evaluate, synthesize, and ethically use information from a variety of sources and media

   c.   evaluate and select information sources and digital tools based on the appropriateness to specific tasks

   d.   process data and report results.

6. **Technology Operations and Concepts**

   Students demonstrate a sound understanding of technology concepts, systems, and operations. Students:

   a.   understand and use technology systems

   b.   select and use applications effectively and productively

   c.   troubleshoot systems and applications

   d.   transfer current knowledge to learning of new technologies

Unit Variations for Younger Students

Set your standards high for younger students so that they can get the most out of this learning experience. The exposure they will get from this unit will broaden their knowledge; however, they may not be able to understand completely the complexity of the Internet infrastructure described in the online tutorials. They are also learning how to navigate online and work collaboratively while learning the Internet concepts.

EXAMPLES

- Choose one online tutorial website to focus on, and teach younger students how to navigate using that particular website (CD Supplement 2A).

- Consider focusing on one or a few of the simple Internet terms for the younger students.

Room Decorations

Decorate the room to make this unit refreshing and fun for everyone. Referring to the room decorations throughout the unit will help students think about how the Internet really works.

EXAMPLES

- Make a large bulletin board labeled "The Internet"; then print out and display a large globe in the middle of the board. Print out several pictures of computers, switches, routers, websites, web browsers, and other Internet terms that you could refer to throughout the unit and attach them to the board around the globe (CD Supplement 2C).

- Make a large spider web using yarn, markers, or string on a poster board and label it "World Wide Web." Attach four or five pictures of different computers on the web.

- Pass out note cards or paper to the students and ask them to write down their favorite website. After reviewing the note cards and checking for appropriate sites, display them on a large bulletin board labeled "Favorite Websites." It may be fun to make one section for each class or grade level.

- Display posters of the Internet framework or World Wide Web around the room.

- Ask the students to draw a picture of what they think the Internet looks like and display their work around the room.

- Using large paper, write a URL that the class uses often, such as a school website, and hang it on the wall.

How the Internet Works

Objective

After viewing online learning tutorials and a slide show presentation, students will learn the basic infrastructure of the Internet and complete a worksheet reinforcing specific terms.

Materials and Equipment

- pencil for each student
- dry erase board and markers or chalkboard and chalk
- yarn (optional)
- note cards (optional)
- computer projection device
- Supplements 2A, 2B, 2C, 2D, 2E, 2F, 2G, and 2H

Supplement List

Below is a list of the lesson supplements that are on the accompanying CD, which is located in the back of this book. Use the CD to open the supplements and modify them, if desired.

SUPPLEMENT	TITLE	FORMAT
2A	Online Tutorials	Word Document
2B	Modem Sound	Word Document
2C	Internet Slide Show	PowerPoint Presentation
2D	How the Internet Works I	Word Document
2E	How the Internet Works II	Word Document
2F	How the Internet Works I Answers	Word Document
2G	How the Internet Works II Answers	Word Document
2H	How the Internet Works III	Word Document

Procedures

Motivation

Students will probably enjoy learning about how the Internet works, so come up with fun ways to share the topic of the lesson with them to kindle their interests. Students may use the Internet at home, school, the local library, or anywhere wireless access is available. But have they taken the time to think about how the information gets to their computer?

EXAMPLES

- Display an animated graphic of the Internet on the projection screen, using one of the Online Tutorials websites (CD Supplement 2A), and talk to students about how information moves from one computer to another.

- Play the recorded sound of a computer connecting to the Internet from the Modem Sound selection (CD Supplement 2B). Explain that this sound is heard when connecting to the Internet through a dial-up modem.

- If possible, take the students on a tour of the school's server room(s). Explain that all of the computers at the school are connected to the server and that the school's server is connected to other computers that are part of the Internet.

- Ask the students, "When you go online to a website, how does that information get onto your computer screen?" Allow several students to share and write their answers on the board. It may be fun to find out the students' ideas of how the Internet works, which also gives you an idea of the general level of understanding in the class.

Purpose

Students will understand the infrastructure of the Internet better when they use online learning tutorials. Indirectly, this lesson will teach students that there are fun ways to learn curriculum online. The online learning tutorials could be their first exposure to an online class. Some students take similar online classes through a home school environment. Many adults even earn a college degree by taking online courses. This lesson will broaden the students' understanding of how the Internet actually works.

Instructional Input

Think about the best way to teach each class about the Internet infrastructure using the online tutorials. Be inventive in how you convey this information to the class. Show the students how to navigate the online learning tutorials by giving step-by-step instructions. You may need to modify the learning tutorial instruction depending upon various students' abilities in the classroom.

EXAMPLES

- Use the computer connected to the projector to show students how to navigate the online learning tutorials (CD Supplement 2A). Some students may not know how to navigate, that is, move the mouse and left click to move the cursor around in a website, so it's important for the teacher or another student to demonstrate how to do this. A student could use that computer to show the class how to navigate while you teach.

- Project the Internet Slide Show presentation (CD Supplement 2C) onto the class screen using the computer projector. It could be used as an instructional tool or simply to get the students to think about the Internet and how it works.

Variations for Younger Students

This may be a student's first opportunity to view an online tutorial. This first experience of using the World Wide Web should meet the needs of all students, which could mean going at a much slower pace while responding to interests and excitement along the way.

EXAMPLES

- Choose one or two of the online tutorials (CD Supplement 2A) to focus on, and teach students how to navigate using these particular websites.

- Show only the first four slides of the Internet Slide Show (CD Supplement 2C) using the projection screen, and save the remaining slides for the World Wide Web lesson.

Check for Understanding

Make sure the students are very familiar with how to open and use the learning tutorials. If students can show you how to do this, then as they navigate independently, they will learn the information on the tutorial relatively easily.

EXAMPLES

- Choose one of the online tutorials (CD Supplement 2A), and have a student use the computer connected to the projector and show how to navigate the tutorial on the screen. This will let you check to see how much the students have understood. A different student could show how to navigate each tutorial.

- Ask the students: "What is the first step to opening the tutorials?" After a student gives a correct response, then ask, "What do you do next?" Allow a student to respond. Continue in this manner until the students seem to understand the process of using the tutorials.

- Have the students explain the importance of knowing how to navigate using the tutorials.

Guided Practice

After demonstrating navigation, explain that students should look closely for the specific terms found on the How the Internet Works I worksheet (CD Supplement 2D) while viewing the online tutorials. During the guided practice, the class will be able to surf the tutorials together to find information.

EXAMPLES

- Write one or all of the terms from the worksheet on the board and use the online tutorial to find the meaning of a term. Then write the meaning on the board next to the word.

- While reading the online tutorial, point out specific terms, and ask the class what that term means. This will help them think about the terms and how to come up with a definition.

Independent Practice

In this independent practice, students will view the online learning tutorials and complete the worksheet titled How the Internet Works I (CD Supplement 2D). Set clear goals so students realize all that is expected of them as they begin navigating the tutorials. As students are working, monitor and help them when needed to maintain a relaxed and positive atmosphere in the classroom.

EXAMPLES

- Have students complete the How the Internet Works I worksheet (CD Supplement 2D) by writing a description of each term in the appropriate box while viewing the tutorials. They may use the illustrations on the sheet as a guide.

- Pair the students in groups of two so that they can work collaboratively and help each other navigate the websites and write definitions.

- Direct students to take notes or outline the information given in the tutorial.

- As students are working, share that the Internet consists of many independent networks connected via routers. A router takes the information from one network and transmits it to another network. In that way, a computer network in New York can route messages to a completely different network in Tokyo, Japan. Network engineers work with routers to make communication between networks as efficient as possible.

Variations for Younger Students

Consider modifying the lesson to meet the learning needs of the classes with younger students. Altering the lesson may help students to understand the information about the Internet.

- Have students complete the How the Internet Works II worksheet (CD Supplement 2E) by drawing a line from the term to the appropriate illustration. Consider completing this worksheet together as a class after students have completed the online tutorial.

- Assign a term to the class on which to focus while exposing students to all of the information.

- As the students hear one of the terms on the tutorial, have them circle the term on their sheet.

- If you are using one website for the younger students, allow them to go to the other learning tutorials if they finish early.

- While viewing the online tutorials, read a few sentences to the class and discuss the meaning of the graphics.

Assessment

A variety of methods could be used to assess this lesson. The method you choose should reflect your teaching style. Ensure that the students are aware of all that is expected of them before the assessment begins to give them the best chance to succeed. This is an opportunity to find out all that the students have learned about Internet infrastructure today.

EXAMPLES

- Go over the worksheets as a class, and ask different students to share their answers. Use the How the Internet Works I and II Answers (CD Supplements 2F and 2G) to ensure students completed the worksheets correctly.

- Collect the worksheets and check them for accuracy and completeness.

- Have students share some interesting trivia that they learned while using the online tutorials.

- Have students explain how the Internet works in their own words. Encourage them to use the information learned in the tutorials.

Extension

Think of ways to expand the students' minds about the Internet and online learning tutorials. These extensions will cause students to think outside the box and further their understanding about the Internet. Choose one of these extended activities, or come up with your own idea to get the students to think more deeply.

EXAMPLES

- Use the How the Internet Works III worksheet (CD Supplement 2H) to give students the opportunity to write several interesting facts that they learned while viewing the online tutorials. This gives students a chance to think in different ways while recalling facts that are interesting to them and on their learning level. Students could share some of these facts with the class.

- Have students research the different endings to URLs (examples: .com/ .edu/ .gov/) and explain the meaning of each one.

- Invite a network administrator to be a guest speaker and talk with the class about the school's network and how it connects to the Internet.

- Use the projection screen to show the class some online learning courses they could take or certificates that they could acquire online now or when they are older. Talk to the students about colleges and universities that offer online certificates or degrees.

- Allow students to learn about other topics using online tutorials. Research and find some fun and interesting online learning tutorials that spark the interests of the class.

- Have the class vote on their favorite online learning tutorial used in this lesson.

- To motivate higher-level thinking, ask students to explain how they think the Internet may change in the future.

Remediation

Some students may need some extra help with learning about how the Internet works. Think of some simple things that could help these students better comprehend the concepts being taught.

EXAMPLES

- Have the students take one or more of the online quizzes available on several of the online tutorials. Supplement 2A contains a list of URLs. The last two URLs contain the simplest tutorials; each one has a quiz at the end. Some of the other tutorials are more advanced and also have quizzes.

- Print out some of the basic facts about the Internet from one of the tutorials and give it to the students to take home and read, or give them a chance to read it in class (CD Supplement 2A).

- Allow students to take the worksheet home to complete it, or allow the students extra time in class, if possible (CD Supplements 2D and 2E).

- Assign students a book to read about the Internet that is on their level and could help them understand how the Internet works.

Accommodation

Be sensitive to students with special needs or disabilities and make modifications to the lesson depending on individual needs. Consider the best ways to modify the lesson to provide the least restrictive environment for these students.

EXAMPLES

- Give these students a copy of the answer sheet so they can study and review the correct answers. It may be difficult for some students to listen and check their work during class (CD Supplements 2F and 2G).

- Allow students with special needs to work at their own pace while learning about the Internet.

- Require that these students only view the online tutorials, not complete the worksheets.

- Pair a special needs student with a partner while viewing the tutorials if it appears overwhelming for the student to work online independently.

LESSON 2

The World Wide Web

Objective

After learning about web browsers and navigating the World Wide Web, students will work together to complete an online scavenger hunt using the techniques learned.

Materials and Equipment

- pencil for each student
- dry erase board and markers or chalkboard and chalk
- old computer parts (modem, hard drive, motherboard) (optional)
- surfboard or picture of a surfboard (optional)
- tape, bell, stickers (optional)
- computer projection device
- Supplements 2A, 2C, 2I, 2J, 2K, 2L, 2M, 2N, 2O, and 2P

Supplement List

Below is a list of the lesson supplements that are on the accompanying CD, which is located in the back of this book. Use the CD to open the supplements and modify them, if desired.

SUPPLEMENT	TITLE	FORMAT
2A	Online Tutorials	Word Document
2C	What Is the Internet?	PowerPoint Presentation
2I	URL	Word Document
2J	URL Cards	Word Document
2K	Website I	Word Document
2L	Website II	Word Document
2M	Scavenger Hunt	Word Document
2N	Website I Answers	Word Document
2O	Website II Answers	Word Document
2P	Scavenger Hunt Answers	Word Document

Procedures

Motivation

Think of a fun motivational activity that will get the classes ready for learning about the World Wide Web today. The following examples will get the students focused on the concepts being taught.

EXAMPLES

- Plan a short class scavenger hunt by hiding a few old computer parts, such as a modem, hard drive, or motherboard, around the room. The first person to locate a computer part wins. Explain that they will be doing a scavenger hunt using the computer today.

- Hold up a picture of a spider web, or draw a spider web on the board. Have students explain why the Internet is called the World Wide Web.

- Ask a few students to stretch yarn across the room to make a web. Explain to the students that information passes through wires from one computer to another. The yarn is a representation of the wires while the students are like computers. The information passes very quickly over the wires to computers. This is a very simple explanation of how computers talk to each other.

- Bring a surfboard into the room (or just a picture of one) and tell the students that they are going "surfing" on the World Wide Web today in class. Ask, "Why do you think it is called *surfing* the web?"

Glossary Terms

navigate. Using a mouse and clicking it to move the computer's cursor around in a website.

URL. Uniform resource locator. A URL is the address of a web page or website.

web browser. Software application, such Mozilla Firefox or Microsoft Internet Explorer, that allows you to locate and view web pages on the World Wide Web.

World Wide Web. A network of web pages that can be viewed using a web browser.

Purpose

As students learn more about navigating the World Wide Web, their understanding will produce intelligent and safe surfing. Often students surf the Internet but do not realize the meaning and significance of some of the navigation buttons on the web browsers or the meaning of the items in a URL. After this lesson, students should be more comfortable using web browsers.

Instructional Input

Plan a lesson that will bring the class to a new level of understanding while surfing the web. Think of the best method for each class to teach them about URLs and web browser navigation techniques.

- Project the Internet Slide Show (CD Supplement 2C) onto the class screen with the computer projector to give the students some basic under-standing about URLs and browsers.

- Pass out the URL worksheet (CD Supplement 2I) and have students fill in the blanks during the slide show presentation. You could also have students fill in the blanks when using the URL cards.

- Print and then cut out the words on the URL Cards (CD Supplement 2J). Write several URLs on the board (leaving lots of space). After writing a website address on the board, have different students tape the cards to the board next to the correct word or symbol. When the students have placed their card in the place they think it should go, review it to make sure the cards were put in the correct places. For added fun, instead of writing the website address on the board, type the address using a word processor and then face the projector towards a dry erase board. Students could show their card to the class and then use a dry erase marker to circle the part of the URL that is on their card.

- Allow students to view a web browser on the projection screen or at their computers while explaining how to navigate using the navigation toolbar/standard buttons. If time allows, show them the differences in various browsers.

- Practice some basic navigation techniques with the class by calling out buttons (back, forward, refresh, home, stop) and then have students click on the correct icon on their computer. It may be helpful to show students how to add and remove buttons to the web browser.

- Write web browser and World Wide Web on the board while explaining these terms.

Variations for Younger Students

EXAMPLES

- Use the computer connected to the projector to show only the last four slides of the Internet Slide Show (CD Supplement 2C) on web browsers.

- Write short and simple websites on the board and tape the URL Cards (CD Supplement 2J) in the correct position. Students may also be able to place the cards in the correct position. Explain the meaning of all of the terms that name each part of a URL. In Supplement 2C, screen 4, titled "URL," each part of the URL is named.

- Draw a simple house on the board to represent the home icon on the web browser. Ask students to find the home icon on the web browser on their computers. Explain to the students that this icon takes you to a specific page called the home page. Continue to draw pictures and teach about other icons on the web browser such as stop, refresh, back, and forward.

- When explaining the web browsers to students, show them only the browser that is most often used in class.

Check for Understanding

Determine the students' understanding of web browsers and navigation techniques. If students do not seem to understand, teach the web concepts again using a different method.

EXAMPLES

- Ask questions, "What is a URL?" "What is a web browser?" What does the backs button do?"

- Ask a student to use the computer attached to the projector and click on certain items on the web browser that you specify. Students could also do the same thing on their individual computers.

Guided Practice

Students should become familiar with how to surf the World Wide Web. Plan an interesting activity to show them how to search for specific information on the Internet to further their understanding.

EXAMPLES

- Show students how to do the scavenger hunt by writing a particular phrase on the board or showing a certain picture that you printed out from one of the online learning tutorials. Then ask a student to come to the computer connected to the projector to search for that phrase or picture on the tutorial. Once the student has located the item, ask another student to write the URL on the board.

- Explain to students how to complete the Website I worksheet (CD Supplement 2K), which could be completed when the scavenger hunt is finished or as homework.

- Have students practice typing URLs in the address bar. Write the URL on the board and ask students to type it into the address bar on their computers.

Independent Practice

This is an opportunity for students to demonstrate their ability to surf the web using web browsers. Think of the best way for students to surf the web to process the information they have learned in this lesson. Organize the class into groups of two or three so that students can work together and help each other. Talk to the class about some collaborative ways they can work together to strengthen their efforts:

- One student can search for the item while the other student writes.

- Both students can use their own computers to search different websites at the same time.

- If using one computer, students can take turns surfing and writing.

- Both students can read the information on the website at the same time.

- Students could search for different items at the same time.

- It may also be a good idea to discuss some rules of working with a partner, so they both take turns while working.

EXAMPLES

- Design a unique scavenger hunt using one or more of the online learning tutorials (CD Supplement 2A). This is one way to complete the scavenger hunt with your class:

  1. Write a specific phrase, word, or fill-in-the-blank sentence on the board that you want them to find using the learning tutorial websites. Make sure this phrase is unique and is located on only one page of the tutorial.

  2. Give a signal, such as ringing a bell, to begin.

  3. Have students work with a partner to locate the correct phrase.

  4. When a group finds the object, have the students stand to show the teacher that they are finished.

  5. Continue writing items on the board for the groups to find one at a time, or write several at a time and have the students write the correct URLs on paper when they locate the phrases. Then the group stands when they have located all of the items.

  6. Give stickers to the group that wins the scavenger hunt.

- Have each group fill in the blanks using the particular website on the Scavenger Hunt worksheet (CD Supplement 2M). The first group to complete the worksheet wins. You could give each person in the group a sticker for winning the scavenger hunt.

- Have students show their understanding of navigation techniques on web browsers by writing the correct term and then describing the function of the term on the Website I worksheet (CD Supplement 2K). This could be completed as groups finish the scavenger hunt or as homework to reinforce the parts of a browser.

Variations for Younger Students

This lesson will need to be modified to meet the needs of younger students. Think of the best way to allow these students to complete the scavenger hunt while reinforcing web concepts.

EXAMPLES

- Have students complete the Website II worksheet (CD Supplement 2L) by writing the correct term in the box using a word bank. Students could complete this sheet with their partner after the scavenger hunt or as a homework assignment.

- Do the scavenger hunt as a class using only one website, and with graphics instead of words. When all of the students are ready, use the computer connected to the projector to show a picture on the screen that is somewhere on the tutorial. Then, the first group that finds the picture using their computer stands and wins. You could give the students a sticker for winning the scavenger hunt.

Assessment

To assess this lesson, reflect on the best evaluation method for determining how much the students understood. The following examples may help to assess students with various learning styles.

EXAMPLES

- Use the answer sheets to check students' work (CD Supplements 2N, 2O, and 2P). Students could share answers in class and check their own work, or the worksheets could be collected and graded after class. Sharing answers in front of the class may intimidate even the most confident student. Ask the class to be sensitive and considerate of students as they share answers from the worksheets.

- Collect and check the URL worksheet (CD Supplement 2I) using the slide show presentation.

- During the scavenger hunt, monitor students to assure that they are working collaboratively and searching to find the information given.

- After the scavenger hunt, collect any written URLs from each group, if required.

Extension

Give students the opportunity to complete a few of these activities to expand their knowledge of the World Wide Web. The following extension assignments could provide some interesting results from advanced students.

EXAMPLES

- Have students research the history of the World Wide Web and explain how it is part of the Internet. They could write a paragraph and present their findings as a class presentation.

- Have students research and explain to the class other items not discussed in this lesson on the web browsers, such as History, Bookmarks, Tabs, Help, and Print.

- Have students type a URL and then modify it to see what happens to the web page. For example, they could delete the text from the URL to show only the domain name.

- Have students design their own scavenger hunt using a particular website and give it to the class to complete.

- Design a scavenger hunt for the entire school with clues located around the campus with questions about web browsers. The first student to solve this scavenger hunt could win a prize.

Remediation

Some students may need extra help in understanding how to navigate using web browsers. Consider the various learning styles in the classroom when students seem to need extra help. Focus on the student strengths and plan remediation techniques that will be effective for your class.

EXAMPLES

- Provide the students with a chance to watch the Internet Slide Show (CD Supplement 2C) a few times.

- Allow students to view the answer sheets (CD Supplements 2N, 2O, and 2P) when completing the worksheet.

- Give the students extra time during the scavenger hunt. If a group finishes early, they could assist other groups who are still working.

- Allocate some extra time for students to review the online tutorials before beginning the scavenger hunt. Students could also review the online tutorials at home a day before the scavenger hunt.

Accommodation

It may be necessary to modify this lesson to meet the requirements of students with special needs. Consider the best way to modify the lesson to provide the least restrictive environment for all students.

EXAMPLES

- A student in an older class could complete the Website II worksheet (CD Supplement 2L) for younger students.

- When completing the worksheets, this student could give the answers verbally to the teacher instead of writing them on paper.

- You could allow the student extra time to complete the work, and/or give the student only a few items to complete.

- When working in groups, you could pair this student with an understanding, patient student.

UNIT 3

Keyboarding

Unit Overview

This unit on keyboarding includes three lessons: Keyboarding Technique, Keyboarding Practice, and Keyboarding Assessment. Keyboarding Technique instructs students on using the correct keyboarding position. Typing using the correct keyboarding position is encouraged in Keyboarding Practice. Keyboarding Assessment tests the students' technique and accuracy according to their grade levels. At the completion of the Keyboarding unit, students should be able to exemplify the correct keyboarding technique and type with greater accuracy.

Unit Goal

To expand students' typing abilities and promote the correct keyboarding position.

NETS•S Addressed

6.   Technology Operations and Concepts

Students demonstrate a sound understanding of technology concepts, systems, and operations. Students:

   a.   understand and use technology systems

   b.   select and use applications effectively and productively

   c.   troubleshoot systems and applications

   d.   transfer current knowledge to learning of new technologies

Unit Variations for Younger Students

Think about the best way to meet the needs of each student in the classroom when teaching keyboarding. For younger students, learning the correct keyboarding technique may be more important than increasing the typing speed. Each class and student should be assessed individually to determine the extent of students' keyboarding exposure, to minimize students' frustration, and to maximize students' potential.

EXAMPLES

   •   Direct younger students to use the Online Keyboarding Websites (CD Supplement 3B) to ensure success. These sites include games and simple typing activities for younger students.

   •   Pair students who are unable to recognize the alphabet with students who know the capital letters.

   •   Simply expose students who are still learning to read to the correct keyboarding position. It may be developmentally inappropriate for some younger students to type for 20 minutes using a typing program.

   •   Consider whether it would be beneficial to have younger students type in all caps instead of having them use the shift keys.

Room Decorations

An inspiring computer lab atmosphere with colorful, interesting decorations can excite students and focus their attention on the keyboarding concepts. Be creative in assembling decorations to motivate students to learn about keyboarding.

EXAMPLES

- Print out and enlarge a graphic of the correct keyboarding position from the second slide in the Keyboarding Slide Show (CD Supplement 3A). Laminate the graphic and display it in the room.

- Create a large poster of the keyboard from the Keyboarding Homework sheet (CD Supplement 3C). This could be enlarged to a 4-foot-long poster, using an enlarging machine, and displayed on a wall or bulletin board.

- Print in color, laminate, and cut several of the Keyboarding Homework Answer sheets (CD Supplement 3E), and display them at each computer or at strategic locations around the room that can be easily seen by the students. Students may refer to this color-coded keyboard sheet while typing.

- Enlarge the keyboard from the Keyboarding Homework sheet (CD Supplement 3C) to make an interactive keyboard. Follow these steps to create a fun keyboard to use in a variety of ways throughout the unit.

    1. Enlarge the keyboard on an enlarging machine two times to create two copies exactly the same size, approximately 4 feet long.

    2. Laminate and display one of the keyboards in the room. To make the keyboard stronger, attach it to a poster board before or after laminating.

    3. Color the keys of the second keyboard to correspond with the colors on the Keyboarding Homework Answers sheet (CD Supplement 3E). Construction paper, paint, markers, crayons, or colored pencils could be used to color the keys.

    4. Laminate and cut the keys from the second keyboard.

    5. Attach Velcro squares or small magnets to the back of the cut-out keys and to the corresponding spot on the keys on the first keyboard.

    6. Attach the colored keys to the large keyboard on display, and remove them to demonstrate the correct fingering positions clearly.

This enlarged interactive keyboard can be used in a variety of ways. If you wish to emphasize only a few keys at a time, add those colored keys to the display. This allows students to see clearly the keys being taught in class. This display could also be used to illustrate the home row keys by adding just those colored keys to the background keyboard. As an exercise, you could pass out the keys and ask students to place the correct keys on the keyboard. After students place all of the colored keys on the enlarged keyboard, you or the students could check it using the Keyboarding Homework Answers (CD Supplement 3E). You could also use this display to illustrate the answers for the Keyboarding Homework sheet (CD Supplement 3C).

LESSON 1

Keyboarding Technique

Objective

After having a class discussion, viewing a teacher demonstration, and using interactive applications, students will work independently to demonstrate the correct keyboarding position and to complete a keyboarding homework assignment.

Materials and Equipment

- pencil and paper for each student
- computer for each student
- poster of the correct keyboarding position (optional)
- plastic keyboard covers to hide characters on keys (optional)
- manila folders (optional)
- computer projection device
- Supplements 3A, 3B, 3C, and 3D

Supplement List

Below is a list of the lesson supplements that are on the accompanying CD, which is located in the back of this book. Use the CD to open the supplements and modify them, if desired.

SUPPLEMENT	TITLE	FORMAT
3A	Keyboarding Slide Show	PowerPoint Presentation
3B	Online Keyboarding Websites	Word Document
3C	Keyboarding Homework	Word Document
3D	WPM Record	Word Document

Procedures

Motivation

A fun motivational activity will set the tone for this lesson and focus the students' attention on keyboarding. Think about an opening activity that will generate enthusiasm for this lesson. Consider a way to connect the lesson to the students' personal lives that will encourage them to pursue typing independently.

EXAMPLES

- Tell a story about two students going to school. One of the students learned to type correctly, and the other student did not think proper keyboarding techniques were important. Have students take turns explaining the advantages for the student who learned to type and the disadvantages for the student who did not learn to type.

- Ask students, "Why should you learn the correct keyboarding position?" Sample answer: Students should learn the correct position so they can type with more accuracy.

- Play the sound of a keyboardist typing and have the students guess the sound. Go to a clip art gallery for this sound effect, or do an online search for "typing sound."

- Discuss with the students the skills they will lack if they do not learn to type correctly.

- Give a keyboarding pretest to view the various keyboarding skills.

Purpose

Provide students with a rationale for learning to type correctly. Explain that it is important to know the correct typing position to be able to type efficiently and painlessly (see Ergonomics for Students in Introduction). If the importance of typing correctly is conveyed to the students in a way that inspires them, they will be motivated to learn the proper techniques. In this lesson, students will learn the correct keyboarding position as well as the correct finger positions when typing. The students will practice keyboarding skills for the next few weeks to become more skillful typists.

Instructional Input

Carefully consider which approach to use for instructing the students on the correct keyboarding technique. Your teaching style combined with the students' current knowledge of keyboarding will determine the appropriate instruction method for each class. Draw on your personal flair to add creativity and excitement to the lesson. Find a way to tap into the students' previous knowledge; this will give them a basis for improving their keyboarding skills. The instructional input should cover the basic keyboarding position and the fundamentals of a keyboard.

EXAMPLES

- Use hanging posters or an enlarged keyboard (explained in room decorations) to teach and reinforce keyboard basics.

- Use the following slides to demonstrate the correct keyboarding position. To use the slides, open the Keyboarding Slide Show (CD Supplement 3A), and project the first slide onto the class screen using the computer projector. Discuss each slide as it is projected, emphasizing the correct keyboarding position and pointing out the various keys on the keyboard.

SLIDE 1: Introduction

SLIDE 2: Title Page—Keyboarding

SLIDE 3: Correct Keyboarding Position

The Correct Keyboarding Position slide (Figure 1) demonstrates the proper way to sit when typing. Click the mouse on the slide to view more information on the bulleted selections.

FIGURE 1. Proper keyboarding position. Encourage correct posture at the computer to eliminate pain and strain, as well as to establish lifelong healthy habits.

- Have the class describe the lady's keyboarding position.

- Have the students demonstrate this correct keyboarding position while sitting at their own computers.

- Walk around the computer lab to ensure that each student is sitting correctly. If a student is not sitting correctly, reinforce the correct position by referring the student to another student or to the picture of the typist sitting correctly.

- Ask, "Why is it important to sit correctly?" Have students raise their hands to respond. Sample answer: It is important to sit correctly so that your arms, wrists, and back are not strained and possibly injured.

SLIDE 4: Home Row

Instruct the students on the home row position. Click the mouse to view each home row key on the class screen. Explain that certain fingers rest on certain keys when typing. Tell the students that the thumbs are always on the spacebar (see the following chart).

Home Row: A S D F J K L ;	
FINGER	**KEY**
Pinkies	A ;
Ring Fingers	S L
Middle Fingers	D K
Index Fingers	F J
Thumbs	Spacebar

- Have the students say the letters as they appear.

- If necessary, repeat the home row keys, and have the students place their fingers and thumbs correctly on their keyboard.

- Explain the reason for the raised bumps on certain keys. The raised bumps will help a typist find the correct home row position by feeling for these bumps without looking down at the keyboard.

SLIDE 5 through SLIDE 10: Keys

Certain keys perform specific functions on the keyboard (see the following chart).

Frequently Used Keys	
KEY	**FUNCTION**
Backspace	Deletes a character to the left of the cursor
Caps Lock	Capitalizes all letters
Delete	Deletes a character to the right of the cursor
Enter	1. Completes a command 2. Moves cursor down to the next line
Shift	1. Capitalizes letters 2. Inserts symbols
Tab	Indents

- Have students explain the function of several important keys on the keyboard. If the students do not know the answer, explain the correct function of the key as listed in the previous chart.
- Have students write these functions on paper or type them into a word processor for future reference.
- Discuss other keys on the keyboard, such as Num Lock, function keys, arrows, Ctrl, Alt, Page Up, Page Down, Home, End, Insert, Print Screen, Scroll Lock, and Pause Break.

SLIDE 11: Great work!

Praise the students for their concentration and participation during the slide show.

Check for Understanding

The students should have a functional understanding of the correct keyboarding position, as well as the basic keys on the keyboard. Be innovative in ensuring that students comprehend this lesson. If the students do not seem to understand these keyboarding concepts, you may need to teach the lesson again in a different way.

EXAMPLES

- Select a student to come to the front of the classroom and explain the correct keyboarding position.
- Point to a key and ask, "What is the function of this key?"
- Play a game in which a student comes to the front of the classroom and reads a question on a card, and then must answer the question to win points for a team.

Sample Questions

- What is the correct keyboarding position?
- What are the home row keys?
- What is the function of the Enter, Caps Lock, Shift, Tab, Delete, or Backspace keys? (Ask this question several times, inserting a different key each time.)

Guided Practice

Contemplate an age-appropriate activity that will give the students an opportunity to practice the keyboarding techniques learned in this lesson. The students will probably have varying levels of expertise depending upon their previous keyboarding experience. If possible, invest in keyboards without letters on the keys or covers for the keyboard. Students will not be able to see the keys and will learn to look only at the monitor. Think of an approach that will allow all students to increase their typing skills at their individual levels.

- Use the computer projector to demonstrate how to use an online keyboarding website to practice typing (CD Supplement 3B).

- Show the students how to use a typing application, such as Type to Learn or Mavis Beacon Teaches Typing, to practice keyboarding, if these are available at your school.

- Have students close their eyes and type the letters that you say. When you are finished, have them open their eyes and read the letters on their screen as you repeat them to check to see if they actually typed the correct letters.

Independent Practice

The students will probably be excited to begin practice on the keyboard. Consider an appropriate method to instruct each class based upon the abilities of the students. Reinforce the idea that speed is not currently important; students should concentrate on developing and practicing fundamental typing skills. Dim the lights as the students type to minimize the glare on the monitors.

EXAMPLES

- Have students practice typing independently using a selection from Online Keyboarding Websites (CD Supplement 3B).

- Have students practice their keyboarding skills using a typing application if one is available at your school.

While Students Are Keyboarding

- Walk around the computer lab monitoring each student, reminding the students of the correct position.

- Observe the students during keyboarding practice to ensure that correct skills are demonstrated.

- If a student needs help, model the correct position and remind the student of the correct position.

- If students are looking at the keyboard, gently place a manila file folder over their hands to ensure that they cannot look at the keyboard. You could also use keyboard covers to cover the keys so students are unable to see the keys.

- If you see frustration on the face of a student, assist the student for a few minutes and encourage the student independently.

- Allow students to refer to a keyboard poster hanging in the classroom if needed.

Variations for Younger Students

Consider an activity that will enable younger students to practice typing at their individual levels.

EXAMPLES

- Carefully choose a typing application suitable for younger students or a website from the Online Keyboarding Websites (CD Supplement 3B).

- Have younger students use the keyboard to type their first names on a simple word processor. This will expose the students to the appropriate use of the keyboard. This may be the first time some students have used a keyboard; typing their names and reading them on the screen will be very exciting!

- Have younger students type the alphabet using a simple word processor.

Assessment

The students have had several opportunities to display their understanding of this lesson's content. Contemplate which assessment method will best demonstrate mastered content on keyboarding, taking into account students' previous keyboarding experience and individual abilities.

EXAMPLES

- Assign the Keyboarding Homework sheet (CD Supplement 3C). Explain that the students will need to color the keys on the worksheet keyboard the correct colors, according to the charts below the keyboard, using crayons, colored pencils, or markers, and answer the question at the bottom of the page. Completing the Keyboarding Homework sheet will reinforce for students the correct finger positions on the keyboard.

- Assign keyboarding practice. Require that a parent or guardian sign the student's homework to indicate that the student did indeed practice typing. If the students are able to connect to the Internet at home, they could practice keyboarding for a certain length of time depending upon ability level using a selection from Online Keyboarding Websites (CD Supplement 3B).

- Give students an option as to which keyboarding practice they will complete for homework.

- Have students practice typing using a word processor, print the results, and turn the assignment in during the next computer class.

- Note student participation throughout class discussions and record it in the grade book.

- Collect keyboarding notes taken during the lesson.

- Have students memorize the position of all keys on the keyboard.

Closure

Commend the students' desire to type correctly. Select a manner for closing the lesson that encourages motivation and praises students for their keyboarding practice. The students should feel special, knowing they have completed an important task when typing.

EXAMPLES

- If there is extra time, review the Keyboarding Slide Show (CD Supplement 3A).

- Remind the class about the importance of typing correctly.

- Ask the students, "What did you learn today about keyboarding?"

- Explain that the next few computer lab lessons will be on keyboarding technique and practice.

Extension

Excitement will probably show on students' faces as they learn to type. A spark may have been ignited in several self-motivated students who really want to type more than the class time allows. Offer activities that will enhance their current typing skills while challenging them. Think of additional ways to teach the students to type correctly while considering the interests and abilities of all students.

EXAMPLES

- Record the students' words per minute (WPM) each class period and then chart their keyboarding progress using the WPM Record (CD Supplement 3D).

- Require the students to spend 15 minutes every day typing at their home computers or to come in before or after school to practice typing. A parent's or guardian's signature could be required to show that the student actually typed for 15 minutes.

- Have students practice typing using various applications and vote for the best typing program.

- Modify the homework assignment by requiring students to color all the keys on the keyboard sheet the appropriate color.

- Organize and administer a typing competition to take place on a certain day. Students may sign up to participate in the typing competition. You could award a certificate to the most accurate and fastest typist in each grade level.

Remediation

Monitor the students to determine whether any are having difficulties in a certain area. Offer students many opportunities to succeed while learning to type. Adapt the lesson to meet the needs of all the students. Consider the best way to train various students having difficulty with typing.

EXAMPLES

- Give students having difficulty a copy of the Keyboarding Slide Show (CD Supplement 3A) to study at home.

- While they are using the typing application, have students whose typing skills need work repeat the same keyboarding lesson several times before going on to the next level.

- Spend extra time showing the home row and the correct keyboarding position to a student having difficulty.

Accommodation

Be sensitive to students with special needs or disabilities and make modifications to the lesson depending on individual needs. Consider the best ways to modify the lesson to provide the least restrictive environment for these students.

EXAMPLES

- Use assistive technology devices, such as specialized keyboards, to improve the functional capabilities of students with disabilities.

- Have students with special needs complete only a portion of the class work and homework assignments.

Keyboarding Practice

Objective

After participating in a class discussion, viewing a teacher demonstration, and using interactive applications, students will work independently to demonstrate the correct keyboarding position.

Materials and Equipment

- pencil and paper for each student
- computer for each student
- various keyboard styles (optional)
- poster of the correct keyboarding position (optional)
- plastic keyboard covers to hide characters on keys (optional)
- manila folders (optional)
- computer projection device
- Supplements 3A, 3B, 3C, 3D, and 3E

Supplement List

Below is a list of the lesson supplements that are on the accompanying CD, which is located in the back of this book. Use the CD to open the supplements and modify them, if desired.

SUPPLEMENT	TITLE	FORMAT
3A	Keyboarding Slide Show	PowerPoint Presentation
3B	Online Keyboarding Websites	Word Document
3C	Keyboarding Homework	Word Document
3D	WPM Record	Word Document
3E	Keyboarding Homework Answers	Word Document

Procedures

Motivation

Plan an opening activity to spark the students' interest and to focus their attention on keyboarding. Devise a motivational activity that connects the students' lives to the concepts being learned. Be creative and try new activities to encourage the students to practice keyboarding.

EXAMPLES

- Collect the Keyboarding Homework (CD Supplement 3C) and go over it with the students.

  1. Have each student place his or her fingers on the Keyboarding Homework sheet to understand visually which fingers are assigned to type which keys on the keyboard.

  2. Say the name of a specific key out loud and have the students place the correct finger on the corresponding key on the homework sheet. This activity allows the students to see that certain fingers go with certain keys on the keyboard.

- Display several different keyboards, such as ergonomic, portable, and bendable, at the front of the room. Hold a class discussion on the advantages and disadvantages of the various keyboard designs. Have students vote on their favorite keyboard.

- Announce that you will award a special keyboarding certificate at the end of class to the student or students who are sincerely attempting to practice keyboarding to the best of their ability.

- Have a guest speaker share personal experiences with typing and discuss keyboarding techniques to motivate the students.

Purpose

Explain that the purpose of this lesson is for students to practice typing using the correct keyboarding technique. It is important to communicate expectations clearly early in the lesson, so that students will be aware of the content and the overall goal. Instruct the students in ways that encourage them to learn on their own. While sharing the purpose of the lesson, make every effort to create a fun atmosphere for learning.

Instructional Input

While teaching correct keyboarding techniques, share your enthusiasm for the subject. This will motivate the students to practice more fervently. Students should feel that you are dedicated to their success in typing and in life. This instructional input will build on knowledge of keyboarding techniques learned in the previous lesson.

EXAMPLES

- Refer to the hanging posters or an enlarged keyboard (explained in Room Decorations) to reinforce the basics of the keyboard.

- Review the correct keyboarding position by opening the Keyboarding Slide Show (CD Supplement 3A) and projecting the first slide onto the screen.

During the Slide Show

- As the slides are displayed, discuss each slide with the class to reinforce the keyboarding position.

- Choose a student to operate the movement of the slides through the slide show by clicking the mouse at the appropriate time.

- Choose a student to "be the teacher" and call on students to answer questions during the slide show.

- Have students write down information from the slides for future reference.

SLIDE 1: Introduction

SLIDE 2: Title Page—Keyboarding

SLIDE 3: Correct Keyboarding Position

The Correct Keyboarding Position slide (Fig. 1, p. 44) demonstrates the proper way to sit when typing. Click the mouse on the slide to view more information on each selection.

Eyes on monitor	Feet flat on floor
Wrists flat	Back straight
Fingers curved	Fingers on home row position

- Give the students a few minutes to write down the correct keyboarding position and then reveal the answer. This will allow the students to self-check their knowledge of the correct keyboarding position.

- Choose a student to demonstrate the correct keyboarding position to the class while sitting at his or her own computer.

- Provide the students with the opportunity to sit correctly. If a student is not sitting correctly, reinforce the correct position by referring the student to another student or to the slide of the lady sitting correctly.

SLIDE 4: Home Row

Review the home row position with the class (see chart). Click the mouse to view each home row key on the class screen. Explain that certain fingers rest on certain keys when typing. Remind the students that the thumbs are always on the spacebar.

Home Row: A S D F J K L ;	
FINGER	**KEY**
Pinkies	A ;
Ring Fingers	S L
Middle Fingers	D K
Index Fingers	F J
Thumbs	Spacebar

- Ask the students to write the home row keys on paper before they are revealed on the slide show. This will allow the students to self-check their knowledge of the home row keys.

- Have students repeat the keys out loud as a class as the letters appear.

- Remind the students of the reason for the raised bumps on certain keys. The raised bumps help a typist find the correct home row position by feeling for these bumps without looking down at the keyboard.

- Discuss why these keys are called the home row keys.

SLIDE 5 to SLIDE 10: Keys

Certain keys perform specific functions on the keyboard (see chart).

Frequently Used Keys	
KEY	**FUNCTION**
Backspace	Deletes a character to the left of the cursor
Caps Lock	Capitalizes all letters
Delete	Deletes a character to the right of the cursor
Enter	1. Completes a command 2. Moves cursor down to the next line
Shift	1. Capitalizes letters 2. Inserts symbols
Tab	Indents

- Give the students a few minutes to list the function of each key as it appears on the slide show. This will allow students to self-check their knowledge on the functions of certain keys.

- Have students describe the functions of the keys in their own words.

- Have students refer to their notes taken previously on the functions of these keys.

SLIDE 11: Great work!

Praise the students for their concentration and participation during the slide show.

Check for Understanding

Plan a fun activity or design a creative way to ensure that students understand the content of the lesson. When asking questions, call on various students and encourage student collaboration. It is important to make individual students feel appreciated and included in the class discussion. If the students do not seem to understand the concepts, you may need to teach the lesson again in a different way.

EXAMPLES

- Have students briefly retell or demonstrate the correct keyboarding position.
- Ask the students, "What is the correct keyboarding position?"; "What are the home row keys?"; and "What is the function of the Enter, Caps Lock, Shift, Tab, Delete, and Backspace keys?" (Ask this question several times, inserting a different key each time.)

Guided Practice

As you demonstrate the typing program, students will sense your passion and become enthusiastic. Inspire students to achieve the next level in typing. Create an atmosphere that allows them to type with confidence. Support your students and encourage the class to support each other. The support and encouragement will become contagious, and students will begin helping other students during the activity.

EXAMPLES

- Use the computer projector to demonstrate how to practice typing using one of the selections from Online Keyboarding Websites (CD Supplement 3B).
- Show the students how to use a typing application, such as Type to Learn or Mavis Beacon Teaches Typing, to practice keyboarding if those programs are available at your school.
- Use the enlarged keyboard (explained in Room Decorations) to demonstrate the correct finger positions.
    1. Call on students to explain which fingers go with which keys. For example, a student could explain which keys the right ring finger is supposed to press.
    2. When students answer correctly, ask them to attach those keys to the hanging keyboard. Students will enjoy working with this enlarged keyboard.

Independent Practice

A calm atmosphere in the computer lab will prepare the students to type. Decide which activity to use for the various classes, depending upon student keyboarding skills. Make sure to give students ample opportunities to succeed. Set high standards and clear goals so students will be aware of your expectations. Dim the lights to minimize the glare on the monitors.

EXAMPLES

- Have students type independently using a typing application or a website from the Online Keyboarding Websites (CD Supplement 3B) to practice skills they have learned. This keyboarding practice could be the same as the one used in the first lesson to review and expand current skills or a different activity designed to broaden the students' skills.

While Students are Keyboarding

- Walk around the computer lab monitoring each student, reminding the students of the correct position.

- Observe the students during keyboarding practice to ensure that correct skills are demonstrated.

- If a student needs help, model the correct position and remind the student of the correct position.

- If students are looking at the keyboard, gently place a manila file folder over their hands to ensure that they cannot look at the keyboard. You could also use keyboard covers to cover the keys so students are unable to see the keys on the keyboard.

- If you see frustration on the face of a student, assist the student for a few minutes and encourage the student independently.

- Allow students to refer to a keyboard poster hanging in the classroom if needed.

- After a period of typing, give the students a break with a few stretching exercises. This will instill the importance of taking breaks while typing.

Variations for Younger Students

Consider an activity that will enable younger students to practice typing at their individual levels.

EXAMPLES

- Carefully choose a typing application suitable for younger students or a website from the Online Keyboarding Websites (CD Supplement 3B).

- Verbally call out one or two letters and have students practice typing those letters over and over again. Do this using different patterns for a couple of different letters.

- Have younger students use the keyboard to type a short sentence on a simple word processor.
- Have younger students type on a word processor using the Caps Lock both on and off to see the function of this key.

Assessment

The assessment method you choose will depend on your style of instruction. Give the students ample opportunities to succeed. Determine the most appropriate means of assessing each class.

EXAMPLES

- Grade the Keyboarding Homework using the Keyboarding Homework Answers (CD Supplements 3C and 3E). When grading, make positive comments such as "Outstanding" or "Great Job!" if the student has earned it. Use the following rubric when grading.

Sample Rubric
Total = 40 Points
One point for each key colored correctly = 37 Points
Three points for writing the home row keys correctly = 3 Points

- As students are typing, observe them to ensure that correct skills are demonstrated.

Closure

The students will find satisfaction in knowing they have typed to the best of their abilities. Be honest with the class, and tell them how they did while typing. Well-deserved praise will encourage the students and bolster their confidence when typing.

EXAMPLES

- If the class worked really hard and everyone was on task throughout the lesson, say something like, "Wow, all of you have exceeded my expectations!" or "I am very proud of the way you tried your best during class today!"
- Explain to the students that there will be a quiz during the next computer class to assess their knowledge about keyboarding.

Extension

The excitement of learning to type and the thrill of competing with other students may invigorate the students to extend their keyboarding practice to outside of class time. Think of various ways to expand the technological horizons of students.

EXAMPLES

- Record and post the students' WPM (words per minute) using the WPM Record (CD Supplement 3D).
- Have students practice to increase their speed and accuracy by using various typing applications.
- Give students a typing assignment, such as copying a poem, a letter, or a recipe, to improve their keyboarding skills.
- Play typing games to motivate students and increase their typing abilities.

Remediation

Throughout the lesson, locate any students who are having difficulty with the content, and modify the lesson for their needs. Strive to be flexible in meeting student needs.

EXAMPLES

- Allow students having difficulties to type at a much slower pace. Remind students that the correct position is more important than speed.
- Ask another student to help show a student the steps to opening the typing application.
- For memorization purposes, have the students name the home row keys in unison 10 times.

Accommodation

Be sensitive to students with special needs or disabilities and make modifications to the lesson depending on individual needs. Consider the best ways to modify the lesson to provide the least restrictive environment for these students.

EXAMPLES

- Permit students with special needs to practice typing using a typing program that takes their skills into account. This could vary from the practice given to the rest of the class.
- Allow students with special needs to look at the keyboard to locate the keys.
- Use a computer-based assistive technology device to assist students with special needs. Certain high-tech and low-tech equipment may facilitate student learning in inclusive settings.

LESSON 3

Keyboarding Assessment

Objective

After having a class discussion, viewing a teacher demonstration, and using interactive applications, students will work independently to complete a keyboarding assessment and to demonstrate the correct keyboarding position.

Materials and Equipment

- pencil and paper for each student
- computer for each student
- plastic keyboard covers to hide characters on keys (optional)
- manila folders (optional)
- digital camera (optional)
- computer projection device
- Supplements 3A, 3B, 3C, 3D, 3E, 3F, 3G, 3H, and 3I

Supplement List

Below is a list of the lesson supplements that are on the accompanying CD, which is located in the back of this book. Use the CD to open the supplements and modify them, if desired.

SUPPLEMENT	TITLE	FORMAT
3A	Keyboarding Slide Show	PowerPoint Presentation
3B	Online Keyboarding Websites	Word Document
3C	Keyboarding Homework	Word Document
3D	WPM Record	Word Document
3E	Keyboarding Homework Answers	Word Document
3F	Keyboarding Quiz I	Word Document
3G	Keyboarding Quiz II	Word Document
3H	Keyboarding Quiz I Answers	Word Document
3I	Keyboarding Quiz II Answers	Word Document

Procedures

Motivation

Design and implement a great opening activity to focus the students' attention on their keyboarding skills. Plan an activity that will motivate students to forget everything else and concentrate on learning keyboarding techniques.

EXAMPLES

- Review the Keyboarding Homework sheets (CD Supplement 3C). Project the correct answers from the Keyboarding Homework Answers (CD Supplement 3E) on the class screen and explain the correctly colored keys.

  When Reviewing the Keyboarding Homework Sheet

  - Ask students, "What are the color patterns?" The students may look on their own papers or on the class screen to locate patterns. Answers: 6, 3, 3, 6, 6, 3, 3, 6; or diagonal steps slanted to the right; or various other patterns found on the keyboard.

  - Go over the answer to the question, "What are the home row keys?" Answer: A S D F J K L.

  - While students are looking at their Keyboarding Homework sheet, encourage them to collaborate and be creative in figuring out some tricks to remember the fingers and their corresponding keys. For example, the left middle finger is assigned to the E, D, and C keys, and DEC is the abbreviation for the month of December. Also, many of the keys for the left index finger sound alike, such as T, G, B, and V. Students will have fun thinking of tips to remember the finger positions.

- Have students open a simple word processing document on their computer. Announce the names of several keys and have the students type the keys without looking at the keyboard. Call out specific sentences or individual letters, depending on the abilities of the class.

- Select a student to "be the teacher" and call out specific letters, words, sentences, or keys, such as Enter and Delete, for the students to type.

- Play a keyboarding alphabet game to review which fingers go on which keys.

  1. Assign each student in the class a letter of the alphabet.

  2. When specific fingers are voiced, such as left pinky or right ring finger, have all of the students with the corresponding key stand. This activity will reinforce for students which fingers go with which keys.

Purpose

Explain to students that the purpose of this lesson is to review keyboarding, practice typing using the correct position, and complete an assessment. Bring the class to an understanding that it is more valuable to learn to type than not to learn to type. Students need to accept the importance of learning to type to gain a sense of urgency to learn. This urgent feeling will drive them to practice until mastery is complete. Give students sufficient coaching and time to practice so that they learn to type accurately.

Instructional Input

First, review the correct keyboarding position. (Skip this step if the students seem to understand the information on the Keyboarding Slide Show.) Next, deliver the keyboarding content, taking into account the various abilities and learning styles. Make every effort to encourage the students in their keyboarding skills.

EXAMPLES

- Refer to the hanging posters or an enlarged keyboard (explained in Room Decorations) to reinforce the keyboard basics.

- Have students create their own multimedia presentation to practice keyboarding skills.

- Review the correct keyboarding position by opening the Keyboarding Slide Show (CD Supplement 3A) and projecting the first slide onto the screen.

During the Slide Show

- As the slides are displayed, discuss each slide with the class to reinforce the keyboarding position and the various keys.

- Choose a student to operate the movement of the slides through the slide show by clicking the mouse at the appropriate time.

- Choose a student to "be the teacher" and call on students to answer questions during the slide show.

- Have students write down the information on the slides for future reference.

- Creatively approach teaching the content in the slide show presentation to ensure every learning style has been taken into account.

SLIDE 1: Introduction

SLIDE 2: Title Page—Keyboarding

SLIDE 3: Correct Keyboarding Position

The Correct Keyboarding Position slide (Fig. 1, p. 44) demonstrates the proper way to sit when typing. Click the mouse on the slide to view more information on each selection.

Eyes on monitor	Feet flat on floor
Wrists flat	Back straight
Fingers curved	Fingers on home row position

- Have the class describe the correct keyboarding position.

- Encourage students to demonstrate the correct keyboarding position while sitting at their own computer.

- Walk around the computer lab to ensure that each student is sitting correctly. If a student is not sitting correctly, reinforce the correct position by referring the student to another student or to the slide of the lady sitting correctly.

SLIDE 4: Home Row

Review the home row position with the class. Use the mouse to view each home row key on the screen. Explain that certain fingers rest on certain keys when typing. Remind the students that the thumbs are always on the spacebar (see the following chart).

Home Row: A S D F J K L ;	
FINGER	**KEY**
Pinkies	A ;
Ring Fingers	S L
Middle Fingers	D K
Index Fingers	F J
Thumbs	Spacebar

- As the letters appear, instruct students to repeat the keys as a class.

- Repeat the home row keys and have the students place their fingers and thumbs correctly on their keyboard.

SLIDE 5 to SLIDE 10: Keys

Certain keys perform specific functions on the keyboard (see chart).

- Instruct students to explain the function of several important keys on the keyboard. If students do not know the answers, explain the correct function of the key as listed in the previous chart.

- Have students review their notes while discussing the functions of certain keys.

Frequently Used Keys	
KEY	**FUNCTION**
Backspace	Deletes a character to the left of the cursor
Caps Lock	Capitalizes all letters
Delete	Deletes a character to the right of the cursor
Enter	1. Completes a command 2. Moves cursor down to the next line
Shift	1. Capitalizes letters 2. Inserts symbols
Tab	Indents

SLIDE 11: Great work!

Praise the students for their concentration and participation during the slide show.

Check for Understanding

Discover a way to encourage each student to become self-assured about learning the content of the lesson. Your liveliness and interest in the material will create enthusiasm for the class in understanding the keyboarding techniques.

EXAMPLES

- Give the students a few minutes to look over their notes or ask questions about the keyboarding techniques.

- Ask the students, "What is the correct keyboarding position?"; "What are the home row keys?"; and "What is the function of the Enter, Caps Lock, Shift, Tab, Delete, and Backspace keys? (Ask the last question several times, inserting a different key each time.)

Guided Practice

This guided practice involves reviewing for a quiz. Consider a method for students to practice the keyboarding techniques, taking their various abilities into account. This practice should prepare the students to succeed on the lesson assessment.

EXAMPLES

- Have students review any notes taken on keyboarding and go over their Keyboarding Homework (CD Supplement 3C).

- Assign collaborative groups to practice and review the information on keyboarding.

- Pair students with a partner to review. Have each student write a few questions from the keyboarding lessons and then quiz a partner.
- Play a game to review the keyboarding content.
- Instruct students to open the keyboarding application of their choice and practice typing.

Independent Practice

Provide students with an opportunity individually to practice the keyboarding skills that will be assessed. This will ensure that the students understand the means of assessment and will promote student success. Clarity is important when explaining the procedures.

EXAMPLES

- Distribute the multiple-choice Keyboarding Quiz I (CD Supplement 3F) to assess student keyboarding knowledge.

  Discuss Keyboarding Quiz I
  - Explain that there is only one answer for each question and the students must select the best answer.
  - If a criterion-referenced answer sheet is used, discuss the correct method for filling in the bubbles on the answer sheet. Give the students a few sample questions.
  - Walk around the classroom and monitor student progress during the quiz.
- Give students a blank Keyboarding Homework sheet (CD Supplement 3C) and instruct them to color the keys appropriately.
- Assess students on demonstrating the correct keyboarding position when typing. Explain the criteria used when observing the students.
- Administer a typing test to determine the students' words per minute. Use the computer projector to explain the steps to completing the typing test.

Variations for Younger Students

Assess each class according to individual learning levels and abilities.

EXAMPLES

- Read Keyboarding Quiz II (CD Supplement 3G) aloud to the younger classes.
- Assess students on demonstrating the correct keyboarding position while typing.
- Instruct students to write the home row keys on a piece of paper and turn it in for a grade.

Assessment

It is a complex task to create a balanced assessment that takes into account the technology standards and the lesson objective while considering the various student performance levels. Different methods of assessment may be given to accommodate the various learning styles.

EXAMPLES

- Use the Keyboarding Quiz I Answers and Keyboarding Quiz II Answers (CD Supplements 3H and 3I) to grade Keyboarding Quiz I and II.

- Record observations on the students' keyboarding position.

- Assess student improvement by giving a keyboarding posttest, which could be compared with a pretest.

- If the typing application used in the lesson has an evaluation component, implement this test as a keyboarding assessment.

Closure

Sum up the lesson by congratulating each person on his or her keyboarding progress and abilities. It is important to allow the students to contemplate their achievements to create a sense of accomplishment within each student. Remind students that while typing quickly is important, it is just as important to type accurately. A big reason for learning the position of the keys is to make sure that you learn to type just as accurately as you write by hand.

EXAMPLES

- Share individual student growth with each student using the WPM Record (CD Supplement 3D).

- Encourage students to practice keyboarding at home using typing software or an online typing program from the Online Keyboarding Websites list (CD Supplement 3B).

- Have a "keyboarding celebration" in which each student receives a certificate for keyboarding practice. Invite an administrator into the classroom to congratulate the students on their typing skills.

- Use a digital camera to take pictures of students typing. Print and display pictures around the room or school.

- Print a sample keyboarding assessment of each student to add to the student's school portfolio.

Extension

Assign an exciting, meaningful activity to students at the completion of this lesson and unit. Be creative in planning and implementing something that the students will never forget.

EXAMPLES

- Encourage students to be creative and design their own keyboard. Have them type a short paragraph explaining the keyboard.

- Have students compose a song that helps them memorize the home row position or the correct finger assignment for keys.

- Hold a class debate on the pros and cons of various keyboard styles and formats.

- Have students create a chart showing individual keyboarding improvement throughout the unit. The students may correlate this chart with the amount of time practiced each day.

- Ask for a student volunteer to be videotaped while typing. The class could discuss various ways the student shows correct keyboarding technique.

- Design an authentic, higher-level assessment for some advanced students in the class. This could require using problem-solving strategies and drawing conclusions on various keyboarding topics.

Remediation

If the teacher senses that a student needs extra assistance, consider the best way to help the student. Watch for verbal and nonverbal clues that a student may exhibit during the lesson indicating that extra help is needed.

EXAMPLES

- If a student seems to have a difficult time grasping a concept, pair the student with another student who seems to understand.

- Allow extra time on the review and assessment for students, if needed.

Accommodation

Be sensitive to students with special needs or disabilities and make modifications to the lesson depending on individual needs. Consider the best ways to modify the lesson to provide the least restrictive environment for these students.

EXAMPLES

- During the review game, it may be difficult for students with special needs to come up with the answers quickly. Give these students the questions a day earlier so they will have extra time to think about the questions.

- Provide a different type of assessment for a student with special needs to determine keyboarding knowledge.

- Modify or shorten the assessment that is given to the class to ensure the success of students with special needs. Grade the assessment using a different grading scale.

- Allow students with special needs to use their notes taken during the lesson.

- Use visual clues to remind students with disabilities when time is almost up during the assessment.

- Provide any necessary assistive technology devices that students with special needs would find helpful when typing.

Note: Throughout the year refer to the typing skills students learned in this Keyboarding unit. Allow students to practice typing when they have extra time to continue keyboarding with increasing accuracy and speed.

UNIT 4

Digital
Citizenship

Unit Overview

This unit on Digital Citizenship includes two lessons: Responsible Use of Technology and Internet Safety and Netiquette. Responsible Use of Technology introduces students to basic ethical issues while using a computer. Internet Safety and Netiquette offers a solid foundation for using the Internet safely and considerately. At the completion of this unit, students will understand the importance of being a responsible digital citizen and know the safe and appropriate use of the Internet.

Unit Goal

To educate students in becoming honest digital citizens while using the computer and to train them in safe and considerate use of the Internet.

NETS•S Addressed

5. Digital Citizenship

Students understand human, cultural, and societal issues related to technology and practice legal and ethical behavior. Students:

- **a.**   advocate and practice safe, legal, and responsible use of information and technology
- **b.**   exhibit a positive attitude toward using technology that supports collaboration, learning, and productivity
- **c.**   demonstrate personal responsibility for lifelong learning
- **d.**   exhibit leadership for digital citizenship

Unit Variations for Younger Students

This unit offers knowledge for students of all ages; however, the presentation of the curricula will differ depending on the maturity of the students. Students are exposed to the computer at an early age and should become aware of some important social and ethical issues concerning the computer as well as Internet safety.

EXAMPLES

- In the first lesson, Responsible Use of Technology, teach only a few of the digital citizenship terms to younger students.
- Teach the second lesson, Internet Safety and Netiquette, over two class periods to allow students more time to assimilate the material.

Room Decorations

An inspiring room atmosphere and decorated bulletin boards will motivate the students and direct their attention toward ethical behavior when using technology. Students will be excited to see the room arranged to display digital citizenship ideas because many of them have probably experienced some of the topics covered in this unit. Be innovative when changing the appearance of the computer lab. The following suggestions may help.

EXAMPLES

- Print the pictures from the Digital Citizenship Cards (CD Supplement 4A), glue them to construction paper, laminate them, and hang them on the bulletin board. Design labels for the cards, if needed.

- Print, enlarge, and display the Family Contract for Online Safety: Kids' Pledge (CD Supplement 4M) to be referred to when the students go over this contract in the second lesson.

- Dedicate a bulletin board or a section of the room to the issues surrounding digital citizenship and refer to the information throughout the unit. Use a banner or letter cutouts to title the bulletin board "Digital Citizenship."

LESSON 1

Responsible Use of Technology

Objective

Students will find the meaning of 11 computer-related terms using an online dictionary and then read an online interactive story concerning social and ethical issues related to technology.

Materials and Equipment

- pencil and paper for each student
- dry erase board and markers or chalkboard and chalk
- dictionary (optional)
- computer projection device
- Supplements 4A, 4B, 4C, 4D, 4E, 4F, 4G, 4H, 4I, 4J, and 4K

Supplement List

Below is a list of the lesson supplements that are on the accompanying CD, which is located in the back of this book. Use the CD to open the supplements and modify them, if desired.

SUPPLEMENT	TITLE	FORMAT
4A	Digital Citizenship Cards	Word Document
4B	Digital Citizenship Slide Show	PowerPoint Presentation
4C	Digital Citizenship Terms Expanded	Word Document
4D	Digital Citizenship: Do's and Don'ts	Word Document
4E	Online Dictionaries	Word Document
4F	Digital Citizenship Worksheet I	Word Document
4G	Digital Citizenship Worksheet II	Word Document
4H	Digital Citizenship Online Stories	Word Document
4I	Mr. J. Thaddeus Toad in "Web Mania" Worksheet	Word Document
4J	Digital Citizenship Worksheet II Answers	Word Document
4K	Computer Security Terms	Word Document

Procedures

Motivation

As students realize that they will be learning about digital citizenship, they will probably be interested in finding out whether things they are doing are right or wrong. Think of a motivating activity that will channel the students' attention toward behaving correctly in all situations in life, not just when using the computer.

EXAMPLES

- Use the Golden Rule to encourage students to think about right and wrong behavior.

  1. Write this quote on the board before class: "Treat others as you want them to treat you." Contemporary English version of Matthew 7:12. (This is the Golden Rule.)

  2. Ask a student to read it to the class, or read it together with the class.

  3. Next, tell the following short story to encourage the students to ponder the issue of right and wrong.

     One day a little girl was working on the computer in the computer lab. The teacher finished explaining the instructions for playing the online Internet game, but the girl still did not understand the way to open the game. You are sitting next to her, and you are already playing the game. What should you do?

  4. Ask students to share what they would do. They will probably be excited to share that they would help the little girl by explaining the steps to begin playing the online Internet game.

  5. Reiterate that students would want a friend to help them if they were unsure of the way to begin the game.

- Allow the students to watch video clips, read stories, and play games while learning about many character traits at a Rising Star Education site called Auto-B-Good, (www.autobgood.com). Auto-B-Good is an Emmy award-winning character education program and has a character development curriculum for schools. Nest Learning is a website listing hundreds more character education videos that you could use (www.nestlearning. com/character-education_c1542.aspx/).

- Talk about the meaning of integrity and why it is important to be responsible for your actions all the time, even when using technology. Explain that if they think something they are going to do could be wrong, it is better not to do it. Discuss the consequences of things that could happen when they are not good digital citizens and may break the law.

Purpose

This lesson will expose students to various ethical and safety issues while promoting positive and conscientious attitudes toward technology. Explain in a way that each group of students will understand that it is important for the student's protection to use technology safely and practice ethical behavior when using a computer. In this lesson, students will build a solid foundation of knowledge to become good digital citizens by learning to use technology appropriately.

Instructional Input

Discuss ethical terms with the students. Think of a creative method to instruct students in the ethical use of computers. Encourage students to have a positive outlook by discussing the benefits of technology. The method of instruction as well as the specific issues focused on during this lesson should be chosen carefully to meet the needs of students at their current levels of understanding and technology expertise.

EXAMPLES

- Use the Digital Citizenship Cards (CD Supplement 4A) to give students something to visualize when discussing the terms. Post all the cards and choose a student to point to the correct card on the Digital Citizenship bulletin board when the definition is given.

- Use the Digital Citizenship Slide Show (CD Supplement 4B) to discuss the terms and their meanings. Ask a student to advance the slides during the multimedia presentation.

- Expose the students to more insightful knowledge regarding each term using Digital Citizenship Terms Expanded (CD Supplement 4C).

- Project the Digital Citizenship: Do's and Don'ts (CD Supplement 4D) onto the class screen using the computer projector, or discuss the do's and don'ts during the slide show presentation.

- Instruct students to take notes on important aspects of ethical technology use. Have them print the notes by hand on paper or type them using a word processor.

Check for Understanding

Students should have a good understanding of the digital citizenship terms and the correct ways to behave when using technology. Creatively prompt students to demonstrate their understanding of ethical behavior when using technology. If the students do not seem to understand these ethical concepts, teach them again using a different method.

EXAMPLES

- Ask students to explain some ethical actions to remember when using computers.

- Ask students to explain some actions that a person should not do when using computers.

- Have students take turns making statements about a person using the computer correctly or incorrectly. The class could give a thumbs up if it is an appropriate use of technology and a thumbs down if it describes an unethical use of technology.

Guided Practice

Research and discussion are the focus of this guided activity. The students are given opportunities to deepen their understanding about digital citizenship. Reflect on the best practice method for each class to help them realize the importance of ethical issues while using the computer.

EXAMPLES

- Choose a student to use the computer connected to the projector to show the class the way to look up a term using an online dictionary (CD Supplement 4E).

- Explain how students can find the definitions using the online dictionaries and record them on the Digital Citizenship Worksheet I (CD Supplement 4F).

- When students have completed the worksheet, discuss each term to ensure each student has written down the correct answer. While reviewing the definitions, incorporate information from the Digital Citizenship: Do's and Don'ts page (CD Supplement 4D).

Variations for Younger Students

You may need to modify the lesson to meet the needs of younger students. They will need more guidance in completing the worksheet and recalling information.

EXAMPLES

- Have younger students use dictionaries to locate the meaning of terms and to match the meanings to the correct terms using Digital Citizenship Worksheet II (CD Supplement 4G).

Glossary Terms

blog. Short for "web log." A website with a person's journal that is usually updated often.

chat room. A virtual room on the Internet used to communicate in real time with other people.

computer virus. A destructive program that spreads from computer to computer, which may be capable of damaging software and/or erasing your files.

e-mail. Short for electronic mail. The exchange of messages using computer networks.

instant messaging. Messages that are electronically exchanged with another person in real time using usernames.

Internet. A worldwide network connecting millions of computers.

podcast. Audio and video files that are downloaded from a website to be played on a computer or a mobile device. The term comes from "iPod" and "broadcasting."

plagiarism. To use someone else's writing and label it as your own or to copy writing from the Internet and use it in your own work without using quotation marks or without naming the person who wrote it.

software. A program designed for use on computers. For example, Microsoft Word or Mavis Beacon Teaches Typing.

videoconferencing. A real time video and audio communication with two or more people in different locations over the Internet.

VoIP. (Voice over Internet Protocol) A real time transmission of voice signals over the Internet.

- Have younger students look up and discuss the definitions together and complete one of the worksheets as a class.

- Expose these students to all of the terms, but focus on one or two terms.

- Hold up an actual dictionary and discuss the similarities and differences with an online dictionary.

Independent Practice

Have students read online safety stories for independent practice. Students need a chance to reflect on the ethical use of computers independently. Think of a way for the class to process the information in a creative and fun way.

EXAMPLES

- Instruct students to choose an online interactive story from the Digital Citizenship Online Stories sheet (CD Supplement 4H) and read it at their computer. The story will reinforce social and ethical issues relating to the computer. Select a student to show the class the steps to opening and navigating the online story website using the computer projector.

- Instruct students to complete the Mr. J. Thaddeus Toad in "Web Mania" Worksheet (CD Supplement 4I) while reading, or after reading, the story.

- Before the students read the online story, ask them to think about the ethical issues concerning technology that are in the story. Write a few questions on the board for the students to answer on paper or using a word processor when they are finished with the story.

Variations for Younger Students

You may need to modify the lesson to meet the needs of younger students who are still learning to read.

EXAMPLES

- Read the online story together using the computer projector and then allow the students to read it themselves by looking at the pictures at their computer workstation.

- Direct students to read the story aloud and look at the pictures with a partner.

Assessment

Throughout the lesson the students have had several opportunities to share what they have learned concerning digital citizenship. Think about the best method to assess each class, and make sure that students are aware of all that is expected of them so that they can be responsible, ethical users of technology.

EXAMPLES

- Use Digital Citizenship Terms Expanded to assess Digital Citizenship Worksheet I (CD Supplements 4C and 4F).

- Use the Digital Citizenship Worksheet II Answers (CD Supplement 4J) to assess Digital Citizenship Worksheet II (CD Supplement 4G).

- Encourage students to share the answers they wrote on the Mr. J. Thaddeus Toad in "Web Mania" Worksheet (CD Supplement 4I), and ask them to discuss the answers.

- Observe the students when they are reading a selection from Digital Citizenship Online Stories (CD Supplement 4H).

- Note student participation during the class discussions.

Closure

The students should now be more aware of ethical behavior while using the computer. Provide them with a few minutes to ponder all that they have learned concerning digital citizenship.

EXAMPLES

- Encourage students to share a story or personal experience concerning the concepts learned about the right and wrong ways to use a computer.

- Ask the class about a computer virus: "How can your computer catch one?" and "How can you prevent viruses?"

- Ask the students, "What have you learned today?" and "How is the Internet fun?"

- Mention that during the next class students will be learning about safety and etiquette on the Internet.

Extension

This lesson has provided a foundation in social and ethical concepts surrounding technology. Think of ways to strengthen the lesson with more advanced questions and activities to meet the needs of experienced computer users. Motivate students to learn more about digital citizenship on their own.

EXAMPLES

- To increase student awareness of computer security, have students record the definition of terms such as encryption, hacker, and password on the Computer Security Terms worksheet (CD Supplement 4K).

- Put the worksheets used in this lesson on a shared folder on the network to allow students to complete the worksheets on their computer workstations. Have them print the worksheets when they are completed.

- Suggest that students think of an interesting digital citizenship question based on the concepts learned in this lesson. They could research the answer using the Internet and present their findings to the class.

- Teach a parent class on ethical use of technology so that parents will understand the meaning of digital citizenship and enforce these concepts in the home.

- Have students search current events to find people who are in trouble for being poor digital citizens, and share this with the class.

- Suggest students interview their parents or another adult and ask them questions concerning social and ethical issues related to technology.

Remediation

Some students may need extra assistance or modifications to the lesson. Watch carefully for students who need help and assist them as needed.

EXAMPLES

- Provide students having difficulties with extra time to read the online stories relating to ethical behavior to reinforce the concepts.

- Spend extra time explaining the Golden Rule and the way it relates to the students' lives.

- Pair students having difficulties with partners to complete the worksheets or online activities.

Accommodation

Be sensitive to students with special needs or disabilities and make modifications to the lesson depending on individual needs. Consider the best ways to modify the lesson to provide the least restrictive environment for these students.

EXAMPLES

- Allow students with special needs to complete only a section of the worksheet.

- Give students with special needs a copy of the worksheet on paper.

- If necessary, read the worksheet out loud to students with disabilities.

Internet Safety and Netiquette

Objective

Students will listen to an online Internet safety song, play an online Internet safety game, read and sign an Internet safety contract, and take the contract home for a parent or guardian to sign. They will also learn more about network etiquette, or netiquette.

Materials and Equipment

- pencil and paper for each student
- headphones for each student (optional)
- laser pointer (optional)
- computer projection device
- Supplements 4B, 4L, 4M, and 4N

Supplement List

Below is a list of the lesson supplements that are on the accompanying CD, which is located in the back of this book. Use the CD to open the supplements and modify them, if desired.

SUPPLEMENT	TITLE	FORMAT
4B	Digital Citizenship Slide Show	PowerPoint Presentation
4L	Internet Safety Song Lyrics	PowerPoint Presentation
4M	Family Contract for Online Safety: Kids' Pledge	Word Document
4N	Internet Safety Games	Word Document

Procedures

Motivation

Begin the class with a fun activity to excite the students and direct their attention toward Internet safety and netiquette. Think of a way to spark enthusiasm in the students while teaching them safe, considerate use of the Internet.

EXAMPLES

- Listen to "The Safe Kids Online Song" (www/safekids.com/safesong/) as a class to enforce the idea of being safe when using the Internet, (Figure 2 illustrates the web page).

FIGURE 2. "The Safe Kids Online Song" web page.

1. Use the Internet Safety Song Lyrics (CD Supplement 4L) on the slide show presentation to follow along with the song or to discuss the contents of the song more closely.

2. Choose a student to indicate the lyrics on the screen using the laser pointer while the class listens to the song.

3. After listening to the song, have students share information they learned from the lyrics.

- Instruct students to listen to "The Safe Kids Online Song" at their individual computers. If headphones are available, students could listen to the song using their headphones as they read the lyrics on the website. Using the computer projector, show the students the steps to opening "The Safe Kids Online Song" (www.safekids.com/safesong/) on the SafeKids.com website.

- Share a story or personal experience concerning Internet safety to encourage students to be safe online.

- Encourage students to share reasons why it is important for the entire family to be safe when surfing the web.

- Tell the class an anecdote to help them understand why online etiquette, or netiquette, is important.

Purpose

This lesson introduces and assesses Internet safety techniques and netiquette. Explain that the Internet is fun but that students should be cautious when online. Emphasize the importance of knowing safe behavior and proper etiquette to become good digital citizens when using the Internet.

Note on Headphones

Remind the students of proper handling of the headphones. Also, show students the way to control the volume and turn the sound on and off. Pass out alcohol cleaning pads to clean the headphones before each use.

Instructional Input

Determine the best method of teaching online safety and netiquette, which could vary for each class. Emphasize the positive aspects of using the Internet and the fun that students can have when using the Internet safely and appropriately. The level of student awareness and understanding of the Internet will indicate the concepts to focus on for each group.

EXAMPLES

- Discuss with the class the Family Contract for Online Safety: Kids' Pledge (CD Supplement 4M). This contract is presented in many of the slide show presentations throughout the book to reinforce these important safety concepts.

    1. Refer the class to their contract as well as the Digital Citizenship bulletin board, if the contract is displayed in the room. To ensure comprehension, have students restate the underlying meaning of the declarations in their own words. Explain that signing the contract means the student agrees to the terms of the contract.

    2. Explain that each student should take this contract home and ask a parent or guardian to read and discuss the contract. Both the parent and the student should sign the contract. If a parent doesn't agree with the contract, he or she can cross out the parts that aren't agreed with or write an explanation on the back of the contract as to why there is a disagreement. The signed contract should be returned to the computer lab during the next computer class.

- Write the term *netiquette* on the board, and discuss it with the students. Netiquette means network etiquette. It is the term for politeness when using the Internet. Remind the students of the Golden Rule and its similarity to netiquette.

Check for Understanding

Students should have a good understanding of the importance of being cautious when using the World Wide Web. Think of a way to determine the students' current understanding of safety and proper behavior on the Internet. If the students do not seem to understand the importance of these concepts, teach the lesson again using a different teaching method.

EXAMPLES

- Ask the students, "Why is it important to be safe on the Internet?" The students could discuss some reasons why it is important to be safe, first with a partner and then with the class.

- Have students define and give examples of netiquette.

- Have students describe how to be a good digital citizen when using the Internet.

Guided Practice

Students will probably be eager to participate in this guided practice because they will be learning the steps to playing an interactive game or activity. Carefully consider which games and activities to do in each class based on student abilities.

EXAMPLES

- Use the computer connected to the computer projector to show the class how to open an activity from the Internet Safety Games list (CD Supplement 4N). These games and activities will review concepts learned in the first lesson, Responsible Use of Technology, as well as introduce new netiquette concepts. Guide the students through the steps for playing the game. The detail of instruction will depend on the grade level of the students.

- As you are explaining, ask a student to move the mouse and show the class the steps to opening and navigating within the Internet safety game or activity.

- Have students list the steps to opening the activity on paper or in a word processing document. Afterward, list on the board the key steps to opening and navigating the game.

Independent Practice

Students will demonstrate concepts they have learned throughout this digital citizenship unit while playing the online safety game and answering interactive questions. The games and activities provide real situations in which the students must determine appropriate responses.

EXAMPLES

- Have students play one of the Internet Safety Games (CD Supplement 4N) or do an activity from this list. If necessary, the students could work with a partner to complete the game or activity. If headphones are available, students could use them while online.

- While students are playing, have them note five important concepts learned about Internet safety and record them on paper or on a word processing document.

Assessment

Throughout this lesson the students have had many opportunities to show their knowledge of online safety and netiquette. When assessing the students, take into account their previous knowledge and abilities.

> ### Glossary Term
>
> **netiquette.** Appropriate behavior while using the Internet.

EXAMPLES

- While students are playing the online Internet safety game, observe them to ensure that they understand the concepts learned in the lesson.

- Ask each student to write the definition of netiquette along with certain Internet safety rules. The students could turn this in to be graded.

- Ask students to turn in their papers with five important concepts learned about Internet safety they noted while playing the game or interactive activity.

- Have students write a paragraph describing the importance of using ethical behavior when online.

Closure

Allow a few moments for the students to think about all they have learned concerning digital citizenship. Students will accept these concepts and internalize them as they realize the social and ethical implications for the proper rules while surfing the Internet.

EXAMPLES

- Review the concepts learned in the first lesson using the Digital Citizenship Slide Show (CD Supplement 4B).

- Play the "The Safe Kids Online Song" and show the lyrics (CD Supplement 4L) again as students leave the class.

- Ask the students, "What have you learned today?" and "How is the Internet fun?"

- Remind the students that they may be able to play the classroom game or activity at home or at the library if there is a computer with Internet access.

Extension

The students may want to learn more about safety on the Internet. There are also many more netiquette concepts that could be discussed. Brainstorm with your students to find out the topics they are interesting in researching. Think of activities to encourage excellent digital citizenship among students.

EXAMPLES

- Have students take the online safety quiz from SafeKids.com (www.safekids.com) to determine their Internet safety knowledge.

- Instruct students to research other Internet safety rules and the importance of these rules.

- Encourage students to research online to find out about e-mail etiquette.

- Have students locate a recent news report of an e-mail scheme, such as phishing attacks, and share it with the class.

Remediation

Think about ways to meet the needs of each student most effectively during the Internet Safety and Netiquette lesson. Monitor the students throughout the lesson, and assist students when necessary. Plan different ways to teach the concepts again to students who need extra help.

EXAMPLES

- Print the slides from the Digital Citizenship Slide Show (CD Supplement 4B) that reviews unit concepts. This will allow students having difficulties to study these concepts more closely.

- Ask students who need the lesson reinforced to listen to "The Safe Kids Online Song" once more to review the lyrics.

- Require students having difficulties to play the Internet safety game or activity for a second time to reinforce the Internet safety concepts.

- Have students who need help work with a partner to play the Internet safety game or activity.

Accommodation

Be sensitive to students with special needs or disabilities and make modifications to the lesson depending on individual needs. Consider the best ways to modify the lesson to provide the least restrictive environment for these students.

EXAMPLES

- Have students with special needs sit in the front of the room next to the teacher.

- Do not require students with disabilities to complete the writing assignment while engaged in the online Internet safety game or activity.

- Provide extra assistance to students with special needs as they launch websites.

UNIT 5

Peripheral Devices

Unit Overview

The Peripheral Devices unit includes two lessons: Peripheral
Devices Basics and Peripheral Devices Identification. This unit
provides students with the foundation and terminology to
discuss and understand various peripheral devices, which are
hardware devices connected to a computer. The Peripheral
Devices Basics lesson will identify and examine various peripheral devices. The Peripheral Devices Identification lesson will
allow students to recognize the peripheral device technology
concepts through evaluation and assessment. At the completion
of the Peripheral Devices unit, students should have a sound
understanding of basic peripheral devices.

Unit Goal

To promote student understanding of technology and accurate use of computer terminology regarding peripheral devices.

NETS•S Addressed

6. **Technology Operations and Concepts**

   Students demonstrate a sound understanding of technology concepts, systems, and operations. Students:

   a.   understand and use technology systems

   b.   select and use applications effectively and productively

   c.   troubleshoot systems and applications

   d.   transfer current knowledge to the learning of new technologies

Unit Variations for Younger Students

Younger students learn differently and are motivated to discover concepts by different factors. Provide younger students with several opportunities to learn about the peripheral devices, taking into account their various learning styles. Reflect upon the most appropriate method to instruct these fledgling learners. The following may help.

EXAMPLES

- Choose one peripheral device website from the four websites listed (CD Supplement 5B, Peripheral Devices Websites) to focus on and teach students how to navigate using that website.

- Concentrate on fewer peripheral devices throughout the unit for the younger students.

- The students could participate in more hands-on experiences by examining the peripheral devices while sitting in a circle on the floor.

- Use a puppet to explain the various peripheral devices.

- Make up a song to a popular nursery tune, incorporating the various peripheral devices. Sing this song with students while pointing to the devices to aid in learning.

Room Decorations

An inspiring room atmosphere and decorated bulletin boards will excite the students and focus their attention on the unit's concepts. Room decorations can generate enthusiasm as well as provide another opportunity to accommodate various learning styles. Be inventive as you plan the room decorations, and remember to have fun!

EXAMPLES

- Print each page of the Peripheral Devices Slide Show (CD Supplement 5A), glue the words and picture to colorful construction paper, then laminate them and hang them on a bulletin board. A banner or letter cutouts could be used to title the bulletin board "Peripheral Devices."

- Cut and glue several of the Peripheral Devices Word Cards (CD Supplement 5H) to large construction paper shaped like clouds and hang them from the ceiling.

- Dedicate a bulletin board or a section of the room to learning the peripheral devices. Refer to the information located there throughout the unit. Set out a few peripheral devices on a table for students to look at throughout the unit.

LESSON 1

Peripheral Devices Basics

Objective

In collaboration with a partner, students will employ critical thinking skills while conducting research. They will summarize knowledge of 26 peripheral devices by doing one or more of the following: illustrate the device, explain the purpose of the device, describing the device to the class, or locating the actual device in the classroom.

Materials and Equipment

- pencil for each student
- dry erase board and markers or chalkboard and chalk
- crayons (optional)
- peripheral devices: Storage Devices— USB flash drive, CD drive, DVD drive, floppy drive, tape drive; Input Devices—barcode reader, data glove, digital camera, fingerprint scanner, joystick, keyboard, microphone, mouse, scanner, trackball, webcam, network card; Output Devices—computer projector, headphones, interactive whiteboard, monitor, network card, PDA, portable media player, printer, speakers (optional)
- computer projection device
- Supplements 5A, 5B, 5C, 5D, 5E, 5F, and 5G

Supplement List

Below is a list of the lesson supplements that are on the accompanying CD, which is located in the back of this book. Use the CD to open the supplements and modify them, if desired.

SUPPLEMENT	TITLE	FORMAT
5A	Peripheral Devices Slide Show	PowerPoint Presentation
5B	Peripheral Devices Websites	Word Document
5C	Peripheral Devices Worksheet I	Word Document
5D	Peripheral Devices Worksheet II	Word Document
5E	Peripheral Devices Coloring Book	Word Document
5F	Peripheral Devices Worksheet I Answers	Word Document
5G	Peripheral Devices Worksheet II Answers	Word Document

Procedures

Motivation

Plan a fun and unexpected opening activity to inspire the students and prepare them for the lesson. A lively event will prompt students to focus on the peripheral devices, and they will be more interested and ready to learn. Design a motivational activity that could be both mentally and physically challenging for the students.

EXAMPLES

- Display for the class the Peripheral Devices Slide Show (CD Supplement 5A) that shows a picture of the peripheral device, then the name of the device. The students could say the peripheral devices that they know. The multimedia presentation could be set to advance each page automatically after a certain number of seconds depending on the grade level. During the presentation, discuss with the class the difference between output and input devices.

- Place the peripheral devices on a table in the front of the classroom. Use as many of the devices as you have to give students the opportunity to see the actual devices. You can use a picture of the devices that you were unable to obtain for this lesson.

    1. Ask, "Who can come to the front of the room and find the speakers?"

    2. Select a student to come to the front of the room and point to the speakers sitting on the table.

    3. Commend the student after locating the speakers.

    4. If the student is unable to locate the speakers, the student could choose a friend to help in locating the speakers on the table.

    5. Continue this exercise with a few of the other devices.

- Play charades or use sign language to communicate with the students about the peripheral devices.

Purpose

Enthusiastically discuss the importance of the lesson content so that students will be aware of the lesson's significance. Explain that the students will be able to name basic peripheral devices and describe their functions by the end of this lesson. Point out to students that knowing the peripheral devices will be of great assistance in the future. It is important to know the name and purpose of basic peripheral devices to understand how computers work. Think of a unique way to provide reasons for learning so that students are able to apply this information to their lives.

Instructional Input

Instruct the students in the use of websites in a way that motivates them to learn. Communicate to the students all that is expected during the lesson including methods of assessment. The students will be excited to begin this Internet activity. Provide encouragement and support to help students discover information on their own.

EXAMPLES

- Using the computer projector, explain navigation techniques for the website and ways to locate the pictures and purposes of the peripheral devices. Become familiar with the websites on the Peripheral Devices Websites list (CD Supplement 5B) ahead of time so that you can decide which sites will best match the abilities of your various classes.

- Explain that this is a student-centered learning activity in which students collaboratively research information and then present their findings to the class. The students could take turns using the mouse to locate the definitions, or they could read the information on the sites and discuss the definitions of devices together.

- Write these important terms on the board and discuss their meanings with the class. Explain the differences among storage, input, and output peripheral devices.

Check for Understanding

Creatively ensure that the students know the directions for this assignment. Reiterate your expectations and the steps for navigating the websites. Insist that all students wait until they hear the word "go" to begin the assignment. This will give you time to be sure that all students understand the procedures and will allow everyone to begin simultaneously.

EXAMPLES

- Have a student use the computer projector to demonstrate the steps for opening the websites.

- Allow several students to show the class navigation techniques among the various websites and methods for locating the peripheral devices.

- Ask the students, "What are you going to do?" The students should explain the steps that they are supposed to follow, which may be: "While working in groups, we will locate each peripheral device on a website, illustrate the device, and write the purpose of the device."

Guided Practice

This guided activity involves student research on the web. You should carefully consider which learning approach will meet the needs of the individual classes. A certain class may require a more structured environment, whereas a self-motivated class could be given more freedom in completing the lesson objective. During this activity, constantly monitor the class's progress. This is especially important because the students are researching on the Internet. Remind the students that if a bad page pops up, they should immediately raise their hands so that you may close it. Even though the school may have a filtering system, some advertisements may pop up that are inappropriate for students. (Refer to the Introduction for more information on filtering the Internet for your school.)

EXAMPLES

- Distribute a pencil and Peripheral Devices Worksheet I (CD Supplement 5C) to each student or group. Clarify that each person will work with a partner to locate, illustrate, and write the purpose of each peripheral device on the worksheet using several websites. The team should incorporate critical thinking skills when determining the purpose of each device.

- Have students create a booklet on the various peripheral devices. Students could work collaboratively or independently to complete the booklet.

    1. Students locate and draw the various peripheral devices on separate pieces of blank paper

    2. Students write the purpose of each device at the bottom of each page.

    3. When finished, students staple the pages together to make a booklet.

    4. Students share their booklets with the class.

- Give the students a choice between the two learning activities, the worksheet or booklet. If students are given a choice, they are likely to choose an activity that best meets their individual learning styles.

Glossary Terms

device. A tool; a machine.

input device. A device used to enter information into the computer.

output device. A devices that receives data from a computer.

peripheral. Separate; able to be attached.

peripheral device. A piece of computer hardware that is connected to a computer.

storage device. A device that reads and writes magnetic disks or optical discs.

Variation for Younger Students

Consider an activity that will enable younger students to learn about the peripheral devices in a fun manner.

EXAMPLES

- Project a certain peripheral device onto the class screen using the Peripheral Devices Slide Show (CD Supplement 5A). The first student to locate the peripheral device on the website and display it on his or her monitor wins. Have the student then say the name of the peripheral device.

- Plan a scavenger hunt using the Peripheral Devices Websites (CD Supplement 5B). Have students locate certain pictures or facts on the websites.

- Have younger students draw an illustration of the device on the Peripheral Devices Worksheet II (CD Supplement 5D) as they locate it on the website, and project it onto the screen so the entire class can see the picture.

- Have younger students could color the picture of the peripheral device in the Peripheral Devices Coloring Book (CD Supplement 5E) after the device is found on the website.

- Allow younger students to navigate on a website to discover pictures and peripheral devices on their own.

- Instruct younger students to work as a class to locate peripheral devices on a website.

Independent Practice

In this independent practice, students share what they know. Decide on an appropriate method of having students explain the purpose of each peripheral device that takes into account their varying abilities. Create a positive atmosphere while encouraging the students to share with confidence.

EXAMPLES

- Display the Peripheral Devices Worksheet I Answers or Peripheral Devices Worksheet II Answers (CD Supplements 5F and 5G) using the projector so that students can self-check their work. Call on volunteers to describe the devices after they've checked their worksheets.

- Use the Peripheral Devices Slide Show (CD Supplement 5A) to display a picture of the device, and then have a student share the purpose of the device.

- Direct each group to go to the front of the classroom to present the purpose of the device. One person could locate the device on the website using the projector, and the other student could explain the purpose to the class.

Assessment

Give students several opportunities to succeed throughout the lesson. The means of assessment should be balanced and effective as well as reflect the lesson objective. Encourage your students as they work; they will be able to do a lot more if they feel you believe in them. Expect more from students, and they will surprise you with all they know!

EXAMPLES

- Observe each group's progress while researching the peripheral devices using the Internet.

- Keep a running record of student participation on the class roll or seating chart sheet to determine individual involvement in the lesson.

- Base the grades on students' contributions to the group or on worksheet accuracy or completion.

- Collect the students' worksheets on peripheral devices for grading and return them during the next class.

Closure

The closing is an important part of the lesson because students are given a few minutes to reflect on all they have learned. This provides students with an opportunity to think about the concepts in this lesson.

EXAMPLES

- Have students share navigation techniques that did and did not work when researching online. This could help students with future Internet research.

- Require students to be accountable for knowing the peripheral devices and their functions. Direct students to review the peripheral devices and their functions for homework.

- Ask the students, "What have you learned today concerning peripheral devices?"

Extension

Assign an extended activity to students or groups that finish early, or allow students to choose one themselves. Be creative in thinking of an advanced assignment for high-achieving students.

EXAMPLES

- Direct students to research more input and output peripheral devices not included in this unit, such as a memory card reader, eye tracking device, Internet phone, Bluetooth headset, or modem. Then, students could illustrate and write a sentence describing the device and present it to the class.

- Take a digital picture of the class or each student in the classroom and post them on a website or print them and hang them on a bulletin board. Talk to the class about the differences between film and digital photography.

- Have students draw a picture of an entire computer system, using at least 10 of the peripheral devices discussed in the lesson. Then ask them to write a paragraph explaining how the devices work.

- Suggest that students write on paper an interesting fact relating to each peripheral device.

- Students could research and create a poster explaining the differences among the media associated with the storage devices discussed in this lesson, such as CD-ROM (Compact Disc Read-Only Memory), CD-R (Compact Disc–Recordable) and CD-RW (Compact Disc–Rewriteable).

Remediation

Throughout the lesson look for students having difficulty and assist them at that time or when appropriate. Classes usually have a wide range of learning abilities. Be sensitive to and aware of all students' needs in your classroom. The class clown may be the student who understands the least, or he/she may be bored and in need of a more challenging project.

EXAMPLES

- While monitoring the groups, provide additional assistance to any groups taking longer to locate the devices on the websites.
- If a group completes the assignment early, ask these students to walk around the room and help other students, if needed.
- Pair students who are having difficulty with the assignment with students who understand it.
- Assist individually, either before or after school, those students having difficulties completing the assignment.
- Call upon another student to explain the concept to the student who doesn't understand. Sometimes it helps for one student to give explanations to another.

Accommodation

Be sensitive to students with special needs or disabilities and make modifications to the lesson depending on individual needs. Consider the best ways to modify the lesson to provide the least restrictive environment for these students.

EXAMPLES

- Require that the students with special needs only view the pictures and information on the website, without writing any information.
- For an assessment, have students with special needs verbally explain the meaning of a peripheral device to you or a partner.
- Ask a co-teacher to sit next to students with special needs and assist them throughout the class.
- Employ assistive technology devices to improve the functional capabilities of students with disabilities.

Peripheral Devices Identification

Objective

After identifying and describing various peripheral devices during a review, the students will demonstrate their knowledge in a peripheral devices assessment.

Materials and Equipment

- paper and pencil for each student

- dry erase board and markers or chalkboard and chalk

- peripheral devices: Storage Devices— USB flash drive, CD drive, DVD drive, floppy drive, tape drive; Input Devices—barcode reader, data glove, digital camera, fingerprint scanner, joystick, keyboard, microphone, mouse, scanner, trackball, webcam, network card; Output Devices—computer projector, headphones, interactive whiteboard, monitor, network card, PDA, portable media player, printer, speakers (optional)

- computer projection device

- Supplements 5A, 5E, 5H, 5I, 5J, 5K, 5L, 5M, and 5N

Supplement List

Below is a list of the lesson supplements that are on the accompanying CD, which is located in the back of this book. Use the CD to open the supplements and modify them, if desired.

SUPPLEMENT	TITLE	FORMAT
5A	Peripheral Devices Slide Show	PowerPoint Presentation
5E	Peripheral Devices Coloring Book	Word Document
5H	Peripheral Devices Word Cards	Word Document
5I	Peripheral Devices Quiz I	Word Document
5J	Peripheral Devices Quiz II	Word Document
5K	Peripheral Devices Quiz III	Word Document
5L	Peripheral Devices Quiz I Answers	Word Document
5M	Peripheral Devices Quiz II Answers	Word Document
5N	Peripheral Devices Quiz III Answers	Word Document

Procedures

Motivation

Create a fun opening activity to help students focus their attention on the peripheral devices concepts being learned. Be energetic and welcoming to the class while turning their attention to the day's instruction. Motivate students by actively involving them in the lesson.

EXAMPLES

- Use the Peripheral Devices Slide Show (CD Supplement 5A) to review the peripheral devices learned in the previous class. Add something new and interesting to the presentation, such as music, animation, or various slide backgrounds.

- Use the actual peripheral device to relate the name and function of the device to the device itself.

    1. Sort the 26 peripheral devices (or as many as you were able to find) randomly, and position them on a table in the front of the classroom.

    2. Ask, "Who can come to the front of the room and find the device that can record a picture using a digital format?"

    3. If the student is unable to locate the digital camera on the table, allow the student to choose a friend to help find it.

    4. Have the student tell the class the name of the device.

    5. Continue this exercise with a few of the other devices.

Purpose

Convey to the class the significance of knowing the basic peripheral devices. Students will work harder to learn these devices if they understand their relevance to future research, work, and recreational activities. Explain that it is important to know the name and function of basic peripheral devices to operate computers successfully. Remember to consider students' various learning styles and abilities when instructing. It will help students to have a clear explanation of the lesson's objective so they will realize all that is expected of them.

Instructional Input

Concentrate on promoting discussion and recognition of the various devices. If you show your enthusiasm and interest while teaching, students will catch the excitement to learn. Think of a way to instruct each class to bring the students to the next level in their understanding of technology.

EXAMPLES

- Give the students an opportunity to teach the class about the peripheral devices.

    1. Distribute to each student a different peripheral device word card (CD Supplement 5H).

    2. Hold up a peripheral device that is on the table.

    3. Ask the student holding the corresponding card to come to the front of the room and explain the purpose of the peripheral device to the class.

- Require that the students select the appropriate peripheral device. This exercise provides students with examples and allows them to come to the correct conclusion.

    1. Distribute to each student a different peripheral device word card (CD Supplement 5H).

    2. Describe the function of a particular peripheral device.

    3. Have the student with the corresponding card locate the correct device on the table.

- Use the word cards to review the difference between input, output, and storage devices.

    1. Distribute to each student a different peripheral device word card (CD Supplement 5H).

    2. Write Input, Output, and Storage in different places on the board.

    3. Ask students, in an orderly fashion, to bring their cards to the board and place them next to the corresponding word that describes the device (input, output, or storage).

- To stimulate higher-level thinking skills, allow the students to write the function and draw a picture of each peripheral device next to the term on paper. Ask students to write whether the device is an input, output, or storage device.

- Encourage a class discussion on the different aspects and interesting facts regarding the peripheral devices, including:

    - Various drives in a computer (floppy, CD, DVD, and tape)

    - Types of compact discs (CD-ROM, CD-R, and CD-RW)

    - Different styles of printers (inkjet, laser, color, and wax)

Variations for Younger Students

Monitor the countenance of younger students to determine their level of understanding. Implement activities that enable students to learn on their individual levels.

- Share with the class several of the colored pictures from the Peripheral Devices Coloring Book (CD Supplement 5E) that the younger students colored during the last computer class.

- Hold up a peripheral device and call on a student with a raised hand to reveal the correct name of the peripheral device.

- Make up stories by giving the peripheral devices lifelike attributes to describe their purpose. Then discuss the relationships among the parts and how they all need to work together like a family to make the computer function correctly.

Check for Understanding

The students should feel confident in their knowledge of the various peripheral devices and their functions. Strive to involve as many students as possible when determining the comprehension level of the class. If the students do not seem to understand, you may need to teach the lesson again using a different teaching method.

EXAMPLES

- Hold up a peripheral device and ask the students, "What is the name of this peripheral device?" or "What is the purpose of this peripheral device?"

- Give the students a few minutes to quiz a person next to them on the peripheral devices and their functions. Monitor the students to determine their individual comprehension levels.

Guided Practice

Plan a lively activity or game that allows the students to review basic computer concepts. If possible, make learning visible and involve all students in the class. Carefully monitor students' progress and amend the activity if needed.

EXAMPLES

- Play a game that requires students to locate the corresponding card and device.

    1. Print and distribute to each student the slides from the Peripheral Devices Slide Show (CD Supplement 5A).

    2. Ask the students to walk around the room and locate the person with the corresponding card and sit down together.

    3. When called upon, each group points to the correct device located on the table at the front of the room.

- Ask various questions concerning the concepts learned in the lesson. Have students work in groups to discuss and then respond to the questions.

- Play a game in which one student states the purpose of a device, and then that student could choose a person in the class to name the peripheral device.

Independent Practice

Think about ways students in various classes can show their knowledge of basic computer concepts. This is the students' opportunity to demonstrate their individual understanding of the peripheral devices and their functions.

EXAMPLES

- Project the Peripheral Devices Slide Show (CD Supplement 5A) on the class screen and have students write on paper the name of the peripheral device as well as the function of the device.

- Hold up one of the Peripheral Devices Word Cards (CD Supplement 5H) and have students write the purpose of the device on a piece of paper.

- Distribute Peripheral Devices Quiz I, II, or III (CD Supplements 5I, 5J, and 5K) to the students depending on their grade level. Explain the instructions at the top of the assessment and remind students to keep their eyes on their own paper. Allow students to practice keyboarding if they finish early.

- Place a quiz on a shared folder, if one is available. Have students open the quiz on their individual computers to answer the questions. Instruct students to answer the questions on the computer and print them out or to write their answers on a piece of paper. Remind students to type their names on their papers before printing.

Assessment

Both objective and subjective methods of assessment could be used to determine student comprehension. Throughout the lesson, evaluate students while they work and participate. Show students that you truly care about them and that you want them to do their best. When deciding the type of assessment, always consider the various learning styles and abilities of the students.

EXAMPLES

- During the objective quiz, monitor the students' progress, and provide assistance if needed. Use the Peripheral Devices Quiz I, II, and III Answers (CD Supplements 5L, 5M, and 5N) to grade the quizzes.

- To stimulate higher-level thinking, require each student to locate and describe on paper the similarities between two peripheral devices, such as speakers and headphones, joystick and mouse, or CD drive and DVD drive.

- Throughout the lesson, make a note of students who participate, and give students participation grades.

Closure

Learning takes place inside and outside of the classroom, so motivate students to learn more about the peripheral devices on their own. Take a few moments to congratulate the students on their accomplishments in learning about peripheral devices.

EXAMPLES

- Encourage students to share a few interesting facts or trivia that they learned about peripheral devices.

- Have students talk about an interesting peripheral device used at home and describe the way the device helps their family.

- Encourage students to share the concepts learned and ways these concepts will assist them in the future.

- Ask the students, "What have you learned about peripheral devices?"

Extension

The excitement of learning about peripheral devices will probably motivate the students to learn more about technology. Students could become actively involved by deciding for themselves which extended activity to complete. Plan additional ways to expand the students' minds and their comprehension of computers.

EXAMPLES

- Using a digital camera, take a picture of each student in the classroom and load the pictures on a shared network drive. Allow students to open their picture and copy it to a blank document. Then have students type a few sentences describing themselves and print it out.

- Create and design a futuristic peripheral device that will help society. Have students draw a diagram and write a paragraph describing the purpose of this device.

- Instruct students to draw a diagram of a peripheral device on poster board and present it to the class, explaining the individual components of the device and how it works.

Remediation

Throughout the lesson be aware of any students who do not seem to understand the concepts. Assist these students during the lesson or at another appropriate time. Consider the best methods of helping students who may need extra help.

EXAMPLES

- Allow students having difficulties to study the peripheral devices as a homework assignemnt, giving them ample time to prepare for the assessment.

- Provide students with extra time to review the terms during class before the assessment.

- Allow students to repeat the function of each peripheral device to each other.

Accommodation

Be sensitive to students with special needs or disabilities and make modifications to the lesson depending on individual needs. Consider the best ways to modify the lesson to provide the least restrictive environment for these students.

EXAMPLES

- Say the name of a peripheral device or hold up one of the Peripheral Devices Word Cards (CD Supplement 5H) and have students with special needs point to the correct device.

- Read the assessment quiz aloud to students with special needs or have these students work with a teacher one on one.

- Require students with disabilities to complete only a section of the quiz, such as the odd or even numbers.

- Employ assistive technology devices to improve the functional capabilities of students with disabilities.

Internet Research and Creativity

Unit Overview

This unit on Internet research and creativity includes three lessons: Internet Research, Slide Creation, and Research Presentations. This unit will instruct students in techniques for researching information, processing it, and presenting their findings to the class, thus creating an authentic learning experience. In the first lesson, Internet Research, students use the Internet to locate and record information on a particular topic. The Slide Creation lesson provides an opportunity to process the researched information and create a multimedia slide portraying the information in a creative manner. The Research Presentations lesson allows students to teach the class about the topic they researched using a multimedia slide show presentation.

Unit Goal

To allow students to conduct Internet research, process information, and report this information to the class using a multimedia slide show.

NETS•S Addressed

3. Research and Information Fluency

Students apply digital tools to gather, evaluate, and use information. Students:

- a. plan strategies to guide inquiry

- b. locate, organize, analyze, evaluate, synthesize, and ethically use information from a variety of sources and media

- c. evaluate and select information sources and digital tools based on the appropriateness to specific tasks

- d. process data and report results

Unit Variations for Younger Students

Give younger students the opportunity to research information with teacher guidance and support. Even though the students may not be able to understand the reason for reading and processing the information, this lesson provides a foundation for future research projects. Completing the lessons in this unit will help younger students increase comprehension skills, expand their understanding of the Internet, and develop multimedia capabilities. You may need to shape the type of research and level of processing for younger students to meet their needs.

EXAMPLES

- To excite younger students and motivate them to learn, choose and focus on a primary theme such as farm animals, seasons, the rain forest, planets, dinosaurs, or children around the world.

- Have younger students complete the research as a class and then discuss as a group the information on the Internet.

Room Decorations

There are many ways to enhance the design of the computer lab to increase excitement and motivate learning. Draw on your own decorating style to focus the students' attention on Internet research. Use the room decorations during the lessons to assign topics or introduce a new skill.

EXAMPLES

- If a theme is implemented for this unit, such as birds, the solar system, countries, or the rain forest, decorate the room with posters and other creative items related to the theme.

- Hang up posters focusing on research or the Internet.

- Design a bulletin board to display information concerning research on the Internet. Create letters or print a sign stating "Internet Research." Print several of the slides that the students create for the multimedia slide presentation and display them on the bulletin board.

- To further enhance the computer lab, change the desktop background for the lab computers to a picture that represents the chosen theme.

- Bring in a caged bird to keep in the classroom during this unit. Allow students to look at the bird and discuss the bird's behaviors.

Note: The supplements and examples for this theme are based on birds; however, the theme may be modified to suit your needs.

Internet Research

Objective

Students will use the Internet to locate and record information on a particular topic.

Materials and Equipment

- paper and pencil for each student
- dry erase board and markers or chalkboard and chalk
- computer projection device
- Supplements 6A, 6B, 6C, 6D, 6E, 6F, and 6G

Supplement List

Below is a list of the lesson supplements that are on the accompanying CD, which is located in the back of this book. Use the CD to open the supplements and modify them, if desired.

SUPPLEMENT	TITLE	FORMAT
6A	Sample Slides	PowerPoint Presentation
6B	Bird Sounds	Word Document
6C	Bird Topic Cards	Word Document
6D	Research Worksheet I	Word Document
6E	Research Worksheet II	Word Document
6F	Bird Worksheet	Word Document
6G	Internet Research	Word Document

Procedures

Motivation

Begin this lesson with a fun activity to promote excitement and learning while using technology. This part of the lesson could be a compelling event or just a motivational inflection in your voice and gestures. A variety of methods could be used to focus the students' interest concerning Internet research.

EXAMPLES

- Show a few sample slides to get students excited about the lesson (CD Supplement 6A). This will begin the unit with the end product in mind.

- If you have chosen a particular theme for this unit, such as birds, rain forests, nature, or weather, play sounds related to that theme. Links to bird audio samples are included on Bird Sounds (CD Supplement 6B).

- If you have decorated the room a certain way for this unit, have students take turns explaining the differences in the arrangement of the room.

- Play soft thematic music in the background as the students enter the room. Ask students to describe the music or sounds they hear.

Purpose

It is important to explain clearly the reason for the lesson so that students will understand its purpose and make the content their own. The students will be using technology to locate information on a particular topic, process the information, and share their information with the class. This lesson is very important in the Information Age because students need to learn how to narrow their focus and locate viable and appropriate resources. Point out that the research will be used to create a multimedia presentation during the next class.

Instructional Input

Determine an innovative method of instructing the classes in Internet research, taking into account their various learning styles and abilities. The length of time it takes to research and narrow the information should always be considered when deciding the method of instruction. Two popular ways of researching on the Internet are visiting a specific website or using a search engine, both of which are explained in the following paragraphs. You may assign some classes to a particular website for their research while allowing other classes to research on their own using a search engine.

EXAMPLES

Examples of Using a Particular Website

- Before class, select a website to be used by the students that suits the chosen theme. More than one informational website could be chosen and used by students to locate facts.

- Use the computer projector to explain the steps to opening and navigating the website.

Examples of Using a Search Engine

- Discuss a sample topic, such as an owl, and explain how to search the Internet for a website about owls.

  - Open the search engine and type "owl facts" in the search box. Then click "Go."

  - Discuss the results of the search with the students and explain that reading the brief summary of the website will help determine whether the site is appropriate for this research activity.

  - Require students to write down the uniform resource locator (URL) and bibliographic information for each website they visit when using a search engine.

Sample Search Engines

www.altavista.com, www.google.com, www.hotbot.com, www.kids.yahoo.com

---

Glossary Terms

search engine. A website designed to search the Internet for a particular topic.

website. A location on the World Wide Web maintained by a group, company, or individual that includes a home page and various links containing information.

Check for Understanding

Creatively elicit student input to determine their understanding of the steps as well as research navigation techniques. Think of a fun way to include all students. If the students do not seem to understand the steps to researching on the Internet, explain the steps in a different manner.

EXAMPLES

- Ask the students to stand if they know the Internet research procedures. Call on one of these students to explain the steps to researching a particular topic.

- State a particular step, then tell the students to show a signal if they know the next step, such as giving a thumbs up or touching his or her own nose. Then call on one of these students to explain the next step.

- Let students take turns explaining the steps to the class. You or a student could write the steps on the board.

Guided Practice

This guided activity involves assigning topics for the students to research. Assign the topics using a fun and organized method, or let the students locate a particular topic from a general theme, such as natural disasters. Consider the various grade levels and classroom management strategies when deciding the manner for assigning topics. Students could work individually or with partners.

EXAMPLES

- Distribute to the students the Bird Topic Cards (CD Supplement 6C), which will show the students a particular bird to research.

- Assign topics and decorate the computer lab at the same time.

  1. Print, cut, and tape to each monitor a different picture related to the unit theme. For the bird theme, for example, display a picture of a different bird on each monitor.

  2. Explain that the picture on the monitor indicates the topic that the student will research. The name of the topic could also be on the card.

- Have students research a general theme to locate a particular topic that interests them personally. This will allow students to develop ownership for their topics.

Variations for Younger Students

Younger students may need a modified guided activity with more teacher assistance. Be sensitive to the needs of these students and design an activity for their ability level that clearly explains the topic they will research.

EXAMPLES

- Assign a class of younger students to the same activity, such as locating a picture of a robin.

Independent Practice

In this independent practice, students conduct Internet research and record information. The manner in which the students organize their research will determine the way the facts will be recorded. Decide the best way for each class to record the facts and clearly explain all that is expected of them. If the students sense that you are confident in their ability to conduct research and determine appropriate facts, they will probably be able to research independently and locate the proper information.

EXAMPLES

- Have students complete Research Worksheet I (CD Supplement 6D), noting the facts and drawing the illustration.

- Direct students to record the pertinent information in notes or create an outline on notebook paper or on a word processor.

- Ask students to draw an illustration on their assigned topic using paper or a graphics art program.

Variations for Younger Students

Younger students will need more structure and guidance. Strive to meet each student's needs. Fledgling learners should be given the opportunity to make their own choices as much as possible when researching; this will engage their interest and promote higher achievement. The following list provides several examples of activities for younger students.

- Have younger students complete Research Worksheet II (CD Supplement 6E), noting facts and drawing an illustration.

- After their research, have the younger students sit in a circle and take turns sharing the things they saw and learned on the website. Draw a simple picture on the board and write a word describing the picture. After hearing their classmates' comments and seeing you draw a picture on the board, the students should be better prepared to complete the writing assignment.

- Have the class navigate the site using their own computers while you read the information to the students or have the students read chorally with you. Then instruct the class to navigate the website and view the pictures by themselves.

- Assign younger students a specific website to allow them to complete the lesson in a timely manner. It would be best to locate a website with audio for students who are still learning to read.

- Ask the younger students to draw a picture on the assigned topic on paper or draw it using a simple paint program.

Assessment

Many assessment methods could be used. You must determine the best manner to evaluate each class. During the lesson, explain the assessment method to give the students the best opportunity to succeed.

EXAMPLES

- Give a similar research assignment for homework, and assign the Bird Worksheet (CD Supplement 6F), where students will write the name of their bird, habitat, migration, diet, life cycle, interesting facts, and websites. You may want to re-distribute the Bird Topic Cards (CD Supplement 6C) to reassign a bird to each student.

- Collect and grade Research Worksheet I and Research Worksheet II. (CD Supplements 6D and 6E). These could be evaluated based on the extent of their completion.

- Observe the students to determine their level of participation during instruction and Internet research.

Closure

Closure is an important part of the lesson because it allows students to process the information learned. Students should feel proud of their work when they have put forth their best effort. The closure could be a quick statement, or it could take a couple of minutes. This is also a great time to remind and motivate the students about the upcoming multimedia lesson.

- Have students take turns sharing various research techniques or hints for quickly navigating the websites. This will allow the students to claim these techniques as their own while helping others learn new gathering tactics.

- Ask students to share one fact they learned about their assigned topic.

- Remind the students that in the next class they will be creating a multimedia slide show on the gathered information.

- Ask students to explain ways that the research concepts learned in this lesson could be useful in the classroom when completing a research project.

Extension

Students are innately inquisitive, and this curiosity may prompt them to research new ideas once they have experienced independent research. Students' access to worlds of information on the Internet with the freedom to explore it will inspire them to generate ideas and think of innovative concepts. Encourage students not only to use the Internet to search for answers, but to help them think about ideas as well. Students will become self-motivated to research more often because it is simple to find the answer to questions when searching online. Think of ways to inspire students to use the Internet research skills learned during this lesson. The following extensions may help.

EXAMPLES

- Suggest that students use other types of media for research, such as encyclopedias on CD-ROM or educational software.

- If a student completes the assignment early, have the student choose a second topic to research or ask this student to help other students complete their research.

- Direct a student who finishes early to create a scavenger hunt on a website for the class to complete. The student types the questions, and then the class uses the website to locate the answer. This scavenger hunt could be on the theme for the unit or on a different topic that the student researched.

- Students could use Google Earth or another map navigation application to locate their bird's habitat or migration patterns around the world.

- Ask the self-motivated student to do a research project on an interesting topic.

- Allow students to go outside to find birds, or look out the window for them, and talk to the students about the birds that live around your area.

Remediation

Some students may require extra assistance throughout the lesson. In addition, students in each class will have various reading, writing, and comprehension levels. Allow students to work at their individual levels while being challenged to learn as much as possible. There are several ways to give students the help they need. Consider the following methods.

EXAMPLES

- Use the Internet Research worksheet (CD Supplement 6G) to give students extra practice and guidance using search engines to locate information on the Internet.

- If students are having difficulties, write on paper the steps to opening and navigating a specific website or just remind them of the steps while working.

- If a student is having trouble using a search engine, provide extra assistance by suggesting phrases to type in the search box.

- Pair students having trouble with students who understand navigation techniques.

- Allow students who are behind on the assignment to complete it as homework or to complete a section of the assignment.

Accommodation

Be sensitive to students with special needs or disabilities and make modifications to the lesson depending on individual needs. Consider the best ways to modify the lesson to provide the least restrictive environment for these students.

EXAMPLES

- Do not require students with special needs to complete the worksheet. Have them draw a picture of the topic instead.

- Ask students with special needs to locate just one fact on the assigned topic.

- If a student is unable to read the text, locate a website that has audio.

Slide Creation

Objective

Students will process their researched information and create a multimedia slide portraying the research in a creative manner.

Materials and Equipment

- bird puppet (optional)
- children's picture books (optional)
- slide show presentation software (see CD Supplement 6H)
- floppy disks or portable storage device (optional)
- computer projection device
- Supplements 6A, 6B, 6D, 6E, and 6H

Supplement List

Below is a list of the lesson supplements that are on the accompanying CD, which is located in the back of this book. Use the CD to open the supplements and modify them, if desired.

SUPPLEMENT	TITLE	FORMAT
6A	Sample Slides	PowerPoint Presentation
6B	Bird Sounds	Word Document
6D	Research Worksheet I	Word Document
6E	Research Worksheet II	Word Document
6H	Multimedia Slide Show Help	Word Document

Procedures

Motivation

Consider a fun activity that will excite students and bring their attention to the lesson for the day. The motivation could include an interesting manipulative, music, or a thought-provoking question. Think about and plan various activities to spark the interest of students of various grade levels.

EXAMPLES

- Motivate students and generate excitement by showing a few sample slides (CD Supplement 6A).

- Play soft thematic nature sounds or music in the background as the students enter the room, or play a few bird sounds using links found in Bird Sounds (CD Supplement 6B).

- Use a puppet based on the unit theme, such as a bird puppet, and talk to the students about creating a multimedia slide.

- Ask the students if anyone remembers the activity for today's lesson, which was explained during the previous class.

Purpose

When students realize that they will create their own multimedia presentation, they will probably be thrilled. Explain that students will use the information from the research worksheets and develop it into a single slide. Students will feel a sense of achievement when they create their own project using individual research and ideas. Each student's personality and unique talents will be expressed by creating individual slides. Explain that this slide will be shared with the entire class upon completion of the project.

Instructional Input

Determine the students' level of expertise when instructing them on creating a slide show. This could be done by simply asking the students if they have ever created a slide show presentation. Be sure to teach the lesson in a way that both includes the students who have already created a presentation and instructs the students who have never created one. Keep in mind the various learning styles: visual, auditory, and kinesthetic. Clearly explain the steps of creating a slide and repeat the steps several times, if necessary.

EXAMPLES

- Use the computer connected to the projector to show the steps of creating a slide. Use Multimedia Slide Show Help (CD Supplement 6H), if necessary.

- Ask the students to repeat the instructions aloud, such as "File—Save As," while teaching the steps of creating a slide.

- To help the students learn the procedure for creating a slide, do a few steps together, with each student using his or her mouse. This will help students process the steps in their minds.

- Have students assist with instruction. A student could use the computer projector connected to a computer to show the class the steps as you explain.

- Go through the process of opening the multimedia application together as a class, so that as you teach, students are able to view the icons and toolbars and follow the steps on their individual monitors as well as on the large screen.

- Use the following steps when instructing students on creating a multimedia presentation.

  Step 1. Create a new presentation. Have students open the application and create a new presentation. If a shared folder is used, have each student open the template and save his or her slide show in a subfolder specified by you.

  Note: If you are planning on making the slides into a class slide show, it is easier to use a shared folder. Members of each class should save their presentations to a specific folder on the network, and then when you create a class presentation, all of the slides will be in the same folder. If you do not have a network and you would like to create a class presentation, you could require each student to save his or her slide to a portable storage device or disk. When you create the class presentation, you could open the students' slides using their disks and put them into one class presentation.

  Step 2. Type information. Students type their name and the information from Research Worksheet I and Research Worksheet II (CD Supplements 6D and 6E). If students have the skill, they could insert a title. The students should consider the font size, color, and style to create an appealing slide.

  Step 3. Insert graphics. Students insert graphics to illustrate their slides. The graphics should complement the slide information. You may show the students the process of going online to locate a certain graphic. Show the students several examples from a book to illustrate that the slides should look proportional.

  Step 4. Use multimedia—animations, transitions, sounds, and backgrounds. Students may animate or add other multimedia elements to one graphic or the text on their slide. Offer guidelines for the amount and type of multimedia effects added to the presentation.

Variations for Younger Students

Carefully monitor the countenance of younger students to determine their levels of understanding. Teach the steps at a pace that promotes achievement for all students.

- Review the steps several times and have students repeat them to ensure comprehension. If the steps are repeated several times during instruction, many of the younger students will be able to visualize the process.
- Create a song to a familiar tune to teach the steps of creating a slide.

Check for Understanding

Students should now have a clear understanding of all that is expected of them as they create their slides. Throughout the lesson, be aware of the students' level of understanding and work to assist the students needing help whenever possible. Think of a creative way to ensure that students understand the steps of completing a slide. If the students do not seem to understand the steps, you may need to teach the lesson again in a different way.

EXAMPLES

- Throughout the lesson, watch and listen to the students and keep a mental record of students who seem to understand and students who may require extra assistance during independent practice.
- Ask a few questions to determine the comprehension of the class.

Guided Practice

Consider the best method for modeling the steps of creating a slide for each class. Individual students or groups of students could teach the class to create a slide; this will reinforce the process of creating a presentation. The guided practice may be implemented throughout the lesson by asking various students to use the mouse connected to the computer projector to demonstrate.

EXAMPLES

- Select a student or students to model the steps of creating a multimedia slide using the computer projector. One student could explain the steps while another student uses the mouse connected to the computer projector to model the steps.
- Pull names from a hat or call out a number. Have the person with that number on the attendance or roll sheet show the class a particular step using the computer connected to the projector.

Independent Practice

As students create their slides in this independent practice, encourage them to be creative and produce a slide that represents the research completed on the worksheets. They will be excited to begin creating a slide that portrays their own ideas and understandings of previously researched material. Students should complete Steps 1–4 as well as choose appropriate colors, fonts, graphics, and backgrounds to illustrate their research. Requiring the students to consider the style of their slide will help them to process their researched information on a higher level. Students are not only writing facts but are processing information verbally and aesthetically, as if drawing a picture.

Step 1. Create a new presentation

Step 2. Type information

Step 3. Insert graphics

Step 4. Use multimedia: animations, transitions, sounds, and backgrounds

EXAMPLES

- Instruct students to complete Steps 1–4 to create their slide. Students type their name, write one or more facts from their research, and then insert a picture. The class could also insert a title, if time allows.

- Direct students to make up a sentence based on the worksheet facts, or type in the fact directly from their worksheet or notes, depending upon the way the facts were recorded.

- Before they animate their slides (Step 4), instruct students to ask another student to read their sentences to check for accuracy.

- Require the students to think about the design of their slides, picture it in their minds, and then begin creating. Choose a children's picture book based on the theme for this unit, and show the pictures to the class. Lead a class discussion on the layout and style of the sentences and pictures. The students could talk about the way the colors and pictures make them feel.

Variations for Younger Students

Think about the abilities of the younger students in the class. Consider ways to stretch their abilities and require them to do all that you feel they can do.

EXAMPLES

- Have younger students insert their name and pictures only.

- Before the younger students begin, have them circle the fact they want to use in their slide. This will help them stay focused when typing.

    Note: This step may need to be spread out over a few classes, depending upon the various abilities of the students.

Assessment

There will be many opportunities for students to demonstrate their knowledge of creating a slide. Think about which assessment method to use for each class. explain to the students your expectations so that they will have the best chance to succeed.

- Observe the class for evaluation and use a mental or written record of student participation.

- If a student was required to check a friend's slide for misspelled words and grammar errors, have the student sign or write his or her name at the bottom of the research record. Collect these sheets and require that each student have a signature on his or her paper for part of the grade.

- Print the slides and grade the students on successful insertion of the information required for their particular grade level.

- Write requirements for the slide or create a worksheet that includes all that should be included on the slide.

Closure

Students will feel proud of the multimedia slide created in class knowing they have done their best work. Give encouragement and compliments to students on a job well done. Provide students with a few moments to reflect on all they have accomplished and learned. Contemplate a way to close this lesson appropriately and prepare students for the upcoming research presentations.

EXAMPLES

- Congratulate the students and give an award to the most enthusiastic learner during the lesson.

- Have students print their slides to be hung on the Internet Research bulletin board.

- Encourage students to share one thing they learned about creating a slide.

- If the students seem to want to create more presentations, explain that in a few months the students will be writing an entire story and creating more than one slide using a multimedia application.

Extension

Think of ways to motivate and inspire students in your classes to exceed the lesson requirements. Students will probably ask if they can create more multimedia shows because they had so much fun creating this one. It is useful and rewarding to get the students' ideas because these contributions can be implemented in an extended class activity on multimedia slides.

EXAMPLES

- Have students learn more about the presentation software used during this lesson using a website from Multimedia Slide Show Help (CD Supplement 6H).

- Have students use HyperStudio or Kid Pix (www.mackiev.com), or a different multimedia slide show application, to create slides.

- If students complete the slide early, encourage them to explore other aspects of the presentation application. These students could then share with the class what they learned.

- Ask the students about the types of multimedia adjustments they would like to be able to do with their slides. This could generate a variety of fun extended activities for the students using different multimedia elements.

- Students could locate and insert the sound of their particular bird to be played when their slide show is played.

Remediation

Throughout the lesson, continually monitor the students to determine whether any are having difficulties with the lesson content. If possible, work with these students to fill in the gaps during the lesson. Sometimes students need to be removed from distractions and focus on the instruction to be successful. There may be students who listen and seem to understand, but when it is time to work they need to be gently reminded of a few steps.

EXAMPLES

- Patiently work with students who need extra help during independent practice. Some students listen and try to understand but are unable to focus or comprehend the concepts.

- If students seem to be talking or playing, rearrange their positions in the classroom before they begin work.

- Have students who complete their slides help students who needs assistance. Throughout the lesson, encourage students to help others sitting around them.

Accommodation

Be sensitive to students with special needs or disabilities and make modifications to the lesson depending on individual needs. Consider the best ways to modify the lesson to provide the least restrictive environment for these students.

EXAMPLES

- Type the research information on the slide to help students with special needs.

- Assign partners to assist students with disabilities during the creation of the slide. Require these students to complete only certain sections of the slide.

- Instruct students with special needs to watch another class's multimedia presentation if unable to type or work independently.

- Implement the appropriate assistive devices to give students needing accommodation the best opportunity to succeed.

LESSON 3

Research Presentations

Objective

Students will first practice and then present their multimedia slide shows on their chosen topics.

Materials and Equipment

- pencil for each student
- sign language book (optional)
- computer projection device
- Supplements 6I, 6J, and 6K

Supplement List

Below is a list of the lesson supplements that are on the accompanying CD, which is located in the back of this book. Use the CD to open the supplements and modify them, if desired.

SUPPLEMENT	TITLE	FORMAT
6I	Presentation Checklist	Word Document
6J	Presentation Record	Word Document
6K	Presentation Grading Sheet	Word Document

Procedures

Motivation

The students will probably be excited about the opportunity to share their presentations with the class. Think of ways to channel that enthusiasm toward learning, using music, hand motions, sign language, or some other creative activity related to making presentations.

- Begin the class in a unique way by using sign language, which will quickly capture the students' attention. The students will be interested and watch intently while trying to figure out the meaning of the signs. Then translate the signs and explain that each student will have a chance to present his or her information using pictures, written words, and sounds (i.e., ways to communicate besides speaking) to create a multimedia slide show. You could also teach them the sign for "bird."

- Act out a simple skit to get the students to think about presentation skills. First, act like a shy and nervous student presenter who is scared to speak in front of the class. Then, act like a confident skilled speaker who speaks clearly and looks the audience in the eyes. Lead a class discussion on proper presentation techniques.

Purpose

Teach this lesson in a way that promotes individuality among students. This will encourage the students' personalities to come forth in their slides and presentations. Explain that each student will present his or her Internet research findings to the class while reading and discussing the information on the multimedia slide. The multimedia research presentations are a great opportunity for students to express themselves and learn new facts from classmates.

Instructional Input

This instructional input involves explaining presentation techniques. Plan a creative way to allow the students to share their slides with the entire class. The students will present their slides using different methods, depending on their grade levels. Clearly explain methods for sharing the information with the class before the presentations begin. The students should be aware of all that is expected of them when presenting.

EXAMPLES

- Distribute the Presentation Checklist (CD Supplement 6I). This will help students prepare for their presentations. Explain this sheet to the students to make sure they understand the steps.

- Discuss with the class the proper presentation techniques and proper audience behavior.

- Have students stand at the front of the classroom or sit at the computer connected to the projector while presenting.

Check for Understanding

Ensure that students understand your expectations during the presentations. The students should be made aware of the need to listen and respond appropriately during the presentations. The students should also understand that they will rehearse their presentations using the presentation checklist before presenting to the class. If the students do not seem to understand the way to present or listen, teach the concepts again using a different method.

EXAMPLES

- Have students explain the procedures for presenting to the class. Select a student to exhibit the correct presentation practices.

- Direct students to explain appropriate behavior during the slide presentations.

Guided Practice

During this guided activity, students will practice presenting their individual slides using the presentation checklist. Observe students by walking around the room while they are rehearsing at their individual computers. Students should need only a few minutes to practice, depending upon the grade level of the class.

EXAMPLES

- To get the students motivated, pass out their original research worksheets. Allow them to review their original notes and drawings, which will refresh their memories on the information they learned during the research. This may help the students during their presentations.

- Think of an innovative method of assigning partners, or have the students pair up with a student sitting next to them in class to practice their presentation.

Independent Practice

The slide show presentations make up this independent practice. Encourage students to relax, have fun, and do their best while presenting. The class should be attentive and focus on the presentation. Remind the students of the Golden Rule, "Treat others as you want them to treat you." Provide structure for the presentations but also allow freedom for the students to express themselves. Remember to be sensitive to students who may be intimidated when speaking in front of the class. Assign a class learning activity based on the presentations.

EXAMPLES

- Instruct students to complete an entry on the Presentation Record (CD Supplement 6J) between each presentation. This will keep the students focused and provide an opportunity for all students to be involved and learn. After each presentation, give the students a few minutes to fill out the Presentation Record, which will allow the next presenter a few minutes to prepare.

- Determine a creative way to call on students to give their presentations, or choose volunteers.

- Invite parents, grandparents, teachers, or administrators to view the class multimedia presentations.

Variations for Younger Students

Younger students will need more guidance and structure when presenting. While considering the abilities and skills in a younger class, think of a way for each student to share his or her information.

EXAMPLES

- Create a class presentation and program the slides to move automatically from one slide to the next. Have the younger students stand or raise their hands when their slide appears in the presentation.

- Direct younger students to read the sentence on the slide from their seats when their slide appears, or have the entire class read the sentence.

Assessment

There are a variety of ways to assess the students during this lesson. Be imaginative when deciding which method to implement. Be sure to inform the students of the assessment method so they will know all that is expected of them. The assessment could be based on their work as well as on their behavior and attitude during the presentations.

EXAMPLES

- Use the Presentation Grading Sheet (CD Supplement 6K) to assess students during and after their presentations.

- Compare Research Worksheet I or Research Worksheet II (CD Supplements 6D and 6E) with the completed slide to make sure that the students used the appropriate information.

- Include student participation during the lesson as well as behavior during the presentations in the grade.

Closure

Conclude this lesson and unit by promoting a sense of accomplishment and achievement for all that the students have learned. The students should feel proud of completing the research, the slide, and finally, the presentation. Each student should have learned something new and experienced a new concept. Take a few minutes to recap by allowing students to share, or choose a different closing activity.

EXAMPLES

- Encourage students to share some of things they liked best about the presentations using the Presentation Record (CD Supplement 6J).

- Have each student draw a star on the Presentation Record (CD Supplement 6J) next to the student's presentation he or she liked the best, or use another method to vote for the most creative slide. Distribute an award or certificate to the student voted by the class as having the best presentation.

- Hang up a few of the best slides on the Internet Research bulletin board and allow students from other classes to view these slides. Students could look at the slides upon entering or exiting the classroom and discuss the differences.

- Compare the final slides' similarities and differences with the original research worksheet.

Extension

This activity has probably excited most of the students in the class; many students will want to create more multimedia presentations. Encourage the students to keep practicing their multimedia presentation skills and learn all they can about the multimedia technology that interests them. Take the time to talk to students who show a real gift for graphic design. Think of creative ways to build technology skills using multimedia presentations.

EXAMPLES

- Encourage students to create their own slides on a fun topic, such as family, dogs, the beach, or anything else that interests them. They could do this at home or at a specific time in the computer lab.

- Start a technology club one day a week devoted to multimedia presentations. Students will enjoy creating these presentations and developing new skills.

- If time allows, share various slide shows from other classes.

- Go on a field trip to the zoo or a local bird sanctuary to view and study birds.

Remediation

There may be students in the class who need a little extra assistance during this lesson. Try to notice these students throughout the lesson and help them when needed. Be resourceful and incorporate other students in the class to assist, if possible.

EXAMPLES

- Pair students who need extra assistance with other students during the presentations. Assist students with their presentations, if needed.

- Allow students having difficulties ample time to practice and prepare themselves before presenting.

Accommodation

Be sensitive to students with special needs or disabilities and make modifications to the lesson depending on individual needs. Consider the best ways to modify the lesson to provide the least restrictive environment for these students.

Give students with special needs the opportunity to participate as much as possible throughout this lesson. Be watchful and sensitive to these students and make adjustments to the lesson to include them.

EXAMPLES

- Read the information on the slide during the presentation.
- Do not require students with special needs to complete the assessment sheets and checklists.
- Allow students with disabilities to use the arrow keys to advance the animation if they are unable to click the mouse.
- Do not require students with special needs to present in front of the class.

UNIT 7

Internet Messaging and Communications

Unit Overview

This unit on Internet Messaging and Communications includes three lessons: Electronic Mail, Instant Messaging, and VoIP and Videoconferencing. The information in this unit provides students with opportunities to communicate electronically using a variety of communication devices. The Electronic Mail (e-mail) lesson gives students the knowledge of how e-mail works and the opportunity to communicate using e-mail. In the Instant Messaging (IM) lesson, students will exchange information with classmates using IM as well as learn the meaning of 20 emoticons and acronyms. The VoIP (Voice over Internet Protocol) and Videoconferencing lesson teaches students how VoIP and videoconferencing technologies work using the Internet, with the opportunity to participate in a VoIP phone call and videoconference. At the completion of the Internet Messaging and Communications unit, students will have a solid foundation of how different types of electronic messages are sent and received using the Internet.

Unit Goal

To promote student knowledge of electronic messaging and communications on the Internet using various hands-on Internet communication experiences.

NETS•S Addressed

2. Communication and Collaboration

Students use digital media and environments to communicate and work collaboratively, including at a distance, to support individual learning and contribute to the learning of others. Students:

    a. interact, collaborate, and publish with peers, experts, or others employing a variety of digital environments and media

    b. communicate information and ideas effectively to multiple audiences using a variety of media and formats

    c. develop cultural understanding and global awareness by engaging with learners of other cultures

    d. contribute to project teams to produce original works or solve problems

Unit Variations for Younger Students

Recognize the abilities of younger students in your class, and plan this unit so that it will challenge yet not overwhelm them. Prepare appropriate activities that will allow younger students to explore ideas while giving them sufficient exposure to the Internet messaging and communications concepts.

EXAMPLES

- Create a take-home booklet of some of the slides from each lesson so that students can read about the Internet messaging concepts and look at the pictures with their parents (CD Supplements 7A, 7G, 7I, 7O).
- Use a puppet to explain some of the Internet messaging concepts.
- Write a song to a popular nursery tune to teach some important communications concepts.

Room Decorations

Do something different in your room for this unit by creating an environment that will excite students about Internet messaging and communications. Find unique Internet communications pictures or hang model satellites from the ceiling to encourage them to think about communications.

EXAMPLES

- Dedicate a bulletin board or section of the room to Internet Messaging and Communications. Print out some of the slides from the slide shows and refer to these posters throughout the unit.

    - E-mail Slide Show (CD Supplement 7A)

    - Instant Messaging Slide Show (CD Supplement 7G)

    - Emoticons and Acronyms Slide Show (CD Supplement 7I)

    - VoIP and Videoconferencing Slide Show (CD Supplement 7O)

- Print out and display some multicultural pictures of students using various communications devices around the world to promote worldwide thinking.

- Display a globe or a picture of Earth to refer to throughout the unit to create visual images reminding students that the Internet spans the entire world.

- In each lesson there is a graph that students will have the opportunity to complete. You may decide to emphasize this graph theme throughout the unit by designing a large graph on a poster board to show the students' favorite type of Internet messaging. Poll students in each class to determine their favorite type of messaging: e-mail, instant messaging, videoconferencing, or VoIP. Then color the appropriate parts of the graph.

LESSON 1

Electronic Mail

Objective

After a class discussion and teacher demonstration, students will share and interpret information about e-mail by sending and receiving e-mail messages.

Materials and Equipment

- paper and pencil for each student
- dry erase board and markers or chalkboard and chalk
- postal carrier costume (optional)
- large envelope (optional)
- mailbox or shoebox
- computer projection device
- Supplements 7A, 7B, 7C, 7D, and 7E

Supplement List

Below is a list of the lesson supplements that are on the accompanying CD, which is located in the back of this book. Use the CD to open the supplements and modify them, if desired.

SUPPLEMENT	TITLE	FORMAT
7A	E-mail Slide Show	PowerPoint Presentation
7B	E-mail Message	Word Document
7C	E-mail Graph	Word Document
7D	E-mail Message Steps	Word Document
7E	E-mail Message Steps Answers	Word Document

Procedures

Motivation

Begin the lesson with something exciting or unexpected that will motivate the students as well as focus their attention on learning about e-mail. Think of a signal, such as ringing a bell, a clapping pattern, or lights blinking, to use with students to prompt them to stop immediately and listen to instructions. This type of active involvement will be especially helpful in this hands-on learning lesson. Explain the signal to the class and practice the signal to make certain they know to stop and listen. Use the signal to get the students' attention for the motivational activity and the rest of the lesson.

EXAMPLES

- Use the E-mail Slide Show (CD Supplement 7A) to introduce students to e-mail concepts and to review Internet safety concepts from Unit 4, on Digital Citizenship.

- Have students explain the similarities and differences between e-mail and "snail" mail.

- Ask students to raise their hands if they have ever sent an e-mail message. Have a few students tell about their experiences.

- Share a personal e-mail experience with the class to personalize the lesson.

- Dress up like a postal carrier with a hat, mail bag, and letters in the bag. Tell the class that you have a letter for the classroom. For added fun you could decorate the envelope and letter with glitter or stickers. With antici-pation, pull out the large envelope from the bag, open the letter and read:

  Dear Computer Class,

  Today you will be learning about a special type of mail called e-mail. This is not regular mail that comes from the post office; it is mail that is sent from one computer to another. You must have an e-mail account to send and receive mail over the Internet. I hope you have fun learning about electronic mail today!

  From,

  (Your name)

Purpose

Show students that this lesson has value for them so that they will be committed to learning. Talk about how popular e-mail has become, almost replacing some other forms of communication. Students should understand how to communicate safely using e-mail. This lesson is an authentic learning experience because students should be made aware of the consequences of e-mail messages. Be creative and energetic when explaining to the students about the relevance of the lesson, so that they can take this information as their own. Discuss with students that they will have the opportunity to send and receive e-mail messages during this lesson.

Instructional Input

Students will be taught how to write and send an e-mail message in this section. Remind students of ethical behavior when sending and receiving e-mail messages. Carefully consider how you would like to instruct the various classes based on their prior knowledge, technological expertise, and grade levels.

- Write the glossary terms on the board and discuss their meaning with the class.

- Discuss how e-mail works by explaining the steps to writing and sending an e-mail message. Show the class these steps on the screen using the computer connected to the projection device. You may want to create a new e-mail address for use in this lesson so that students are not reading your personal e-mail messages.

  Steps to Writing and Sending an E-mail Message:
  1. Log in to your e-mail client account.
  2. Click Compose Mail or New Mail.
  3. Fill in the Header.
     a. To: Type the recipient's e-mail address.
     b. Subject: Type a short statement describing the message's content.
     c. CC: Type an e-mail address of someone you want to receive a copy of the message.
     d. BCC: Type an e-mail address of someone you want to receive a copy of the message without anyone else seeing the person's e-mail address.
  4. Write your message in the large space provided. Don't use any private information, unless you encrypt it. Anyone can read your e-mail message when it is sent using clear text via the Internet. Remind your students to NEVER send passwords, credit card numbers, or any other sensitive information via email without first encrypting the data. Malicious hackers can easily see plain text and can obtain your information when you send it over the Internet.
  5. Click Send.
  6. The message goes over the Internet to an e-mail server, and then to the recipient.

- Draw a picture on the board of two computers with an e-mail server between them. Talk about how the e-mail message goes from one computer to another through an e-mail server.

- Have three volunteers stand in front of the classroom to act out how an e-mail message is sent over the Internet. Two students can be computers while the student standing between them is the e-mail server. Give one of the students acting as a computer an envelope that represents an e-mail message. This student then passes the envelope to the student standing as an e-mail server. Then, that student passes the envelope to the other computer. Talk to the class about how the computers are able to read, interpret, and send the message to the specific e-mail address written in the header information.

Check for Understanding

Watch the students carefully to determine their comprehension concerning e-mail messages. Ask questions to determine whether the students have a clear understanding about e-mail messages. If students seem not to understand, you may need to teach the class about e-mail again using a different method.

EXAMPLES

- Ask the students, "What is an e-mail message, e-mail client, e-mail server, and e-mail address?"

- Have the students explain the importance of being safe and smart when using e-mail.

- Ask a student to explain how to send an e-mail message to a friend.

Glossary Terms

e-mail. E-mail is short for electronic mail, the transmission of messages over communications networks.

e-mail address. An electronic postal address with a username and domain name. (Example: username@yahoo.com)

e-mail client. Software that allows you to create an account to send and receive e-mail messages. (Examples: Microsoft Outlook, Yahoo, Gmail, or AOL)

e-mail server. A computer used to send e-mail that works as an Internet post office.

encrypt. To change regular language into codes. This is done by your e-mail server.

reply. In e-mail, to answer a person who sent you an e-mail by writing a note back to the person.

Guided Practice

In this guided activity, students will send and receive e-mail as a class. You may already have e-mail accounts assigned to students. If not, you may decide to create e-mail accounts for students to use in this lesson depending upon the abilities of students in the class. Carefully consider the best way for each class to experience e-mail using individual e-mail accounts or one class account.

EXAMPLES

- Allow various students to use the computer connected to the projector to show the steps of writing and sending an e-mail, as well as opening and replying to an e-mail message sent to your account. This activity will give students the opportunity to practice writing, sending, and opening e-mail messages and allow the class to see the steps.

  Steps of Opening and Replying to an E-mail Message:
  1. Log in to your e-mail client account.
  2. Click Inbox.
  3. Click on the message that you want to open.

4. Read the message. If needed, click:

- Reply—Allows you to reply (to answer by writing a note) to the person with the same e-mail address.

- Forward—Allows you to send the message to someone with another e-mail address.

- Attachment—Allows you to open a file sent with the e-mail message. Don't open any attachments if you don't know who sent them. The attachment could contain a virus that could harm your computer.

5. Click Send.

- If students have been assigned their own e-mail accounts, allow a student to log in to his or her account, using the computer connected to the projector, to show the class these steps. Students could practice by sending you an e-mail message with their name and the title of their favorite song.

Variations for Younger Students

Consider the following ways to modify this lesson to meet the needs of younger students.

EXAMPLES

- Fill in blanks on the E-mail Message worksheet (CD Supplement 7B), which shows students the information needed to send an e-mail message. Have students write a message to the principal about their favorite school activity. You could choose one student's worksheet to send to the principal, using your e-mail account and the computer connected to the projector, while students watch on the class computer screen.

- Create an e-mail account to use for your class, and use the computer projector to show students step by step the procedure for sending and receiving e-mail. The entire class may be able to log in to that same account on their individual computers, which will give them an opportunity to see the e-mail client on their own computer.

- Ask a student to use the computer connected to the projector and to show the steps of opening an e-mail and writing an e-mail as you tell the student what to do. For added fun, send a message to the class and have a student open the message with a subject labeled "secret message." Write something special to the class in the message such as, "Keep reaching for the stars," or "Treat others as you would have them treat you."

- Draw the "@" symbol on the board and discuss the differences between a website address (www.yahoo.com) and an e-mail address (username@yahoo.com).

- Bring in a mailbox or make one out of a shoebox and allow students to write a message on paper and put it into the mailbox to send to a friend. Have a student dress up like a mail carrier and another student put a letter in the pretend mailbox. The mail carrier gets the letter and then takes it to the post office. The person at the "post office" reads the name on the letter and takes it to the person in the classroom.

Independent Practice

After students have had a chance to practice sending and receiving e-mail, this is their chance to work independently with e-mail messages while being closely monitored. Carefully decide what you would like each class to be able to do independently. Some classes could send and receive e-mail while working independently, while other classes should work collaboratively. This is the students' opportunity to synthesize all that they have learned about e-mail. Consider reminding students that anything they write in an e-mail message can be printed out, and it is best to be very nice when writing so they do not offend another person.

Glossary Terms

clear text. Text or data sent electronically that can be read by anyone. Also called plain text.

encryption. Coding your message into a secret code.

spam. Unsolicited e-mail that is sent to many people at one time.

unsolicited. An e-mail that was not requested.

EXAMPLES

- Send and receive e-mail from at least five other students in order to fill in a graph on the E-mail Graph worksheet (CD Supplement 7C). The graph illustrates the amount of time students spend checking and sending e-mails every day.

- Have students arrange the steps to writing and sending an e-mail in the correct order on the E-mail Message Steps worksheet (CD Supplement 7D) by writing the correct number next to the corresponding step.

- Instruct students to write on a piece of paper the steps of writing and sending an e-mail message.

- Call upon different students to explain how to write and send an e-mail message. When students give the correct step, they could go to the computer connected to the projector and perform the step for the class to see. Continue in this manner until everyone has a chance to come to the computer to complete a step.

- Ask students to write down at least three proper e-mail etiquette techniques when writing and opening e-mail.

- Have students make up their own e-mail address and write it on a piece of paper. Students could share their addresses with the class.

Assessment

Throughout the lesson provide ample opportunities for students to learn the information about e-mail as well as practice all that they have learned. Communicate clearly your expectations so that students understand all that is expected of them so that they can be successful.

EXAMPLES

- Use the E-mail Message Steps Answers (CD Supplement 7E) to assess student accuracy on the worksheet.

- Collect and assess the E-mail Graph worksheets (CD Supplement 7C) for completeness.

- Have students write or share the meanings of the following terms discussed in this lesson: e-mail message, e-mail client, e-mail server, and e-mail address.

- As the students are working, observe and record each student's progress on a class roster or seating chart.

- Have students print at least one of their e-mail messages so you can see they have filled in correctly all of the information you required. This will also give students the opportunity of seeing their e-mail messages in a printed format.

Closure

Provide closure to the lesson by giving students the opportunity to share some things about Internet messaging and communications that they learned during the lesson. This allows students to process and reflect upon all that they have learned about e-mail communications.

EXAMPLES

- Have students share one thing that they learned about e-mail with a partner sitting next to them.

- Ask, "What have you learned today?"

- Allow students to send you an e-mail message telling one thing that they learned that day about communication using e-mail.

Extension

Continue the e-mail excitement by challenging students to complete another e-mail communications activity. Choose one of these activities, or plan your own to motivate and move students in your classes to the next level while learning about Internet communications.

EXAMPLES

- Create e-pals with your classes and provide a few minutes at a scheduled time for students to check and send e-mail with their e-pals. You could create assignments on information that they must find out from their e-pal or give them a specific topic to write about. You may decide to assign e-pals within your school, or with another school, if you can find a teacher who you can work closely with. It may even be possible to find a teacher located in a different school district or even a different country to promote cultural learning experiences and broaden your students' global awareness. You may want to use a website that connects teachers and students, such as ePals (www.epals.com).

- Discuss the different header options associated with an e-mail message, such as: high importance, low importance, flag, font, sent mail, drafts, deleted items, and reply to all.

- Have students research and then present information to the class concerning methods hackers use to locate, find, and open e-mail messages to gather personal information.

- Have students research various types of spam (junk e-mail) and phishing attacks (tricking someone into e-mailing confidential information or tricking them into doing something that they normally wouldn't do) and share recent news stories about how people have been tricked.

- Do a report explaining the reason why junk e-mail messages are called spam.

- Communicate with students using e-mail. Students must check their e-mail upon arriving in the classroom to see the assignment for the day.

- Have students research to discover when the first recorded e-mail was sent.

Remediation

Monitor students closely throughout the lesson to see if anyone is struggling or needs a little extra help. Consider one of the following examples to provide students with the practice needed to complete the lesson.

EXAMPLES

- Give the students a handout of detailed steps for writing, sending, and opening an e-mail message.

- Pair students having difficulty with a partner who seems to understand the e-mail activity. Sometimes it helps to have one student explain the assignment to another student.

- Give students extra time when writing an e-mail message or completing an activity, to promote success among students.

Accommodation

Be sensitive to students with special needs or disabilities and make modifications to the lesson depending on individual needs. Consider the best ways to modify the lesson to provide the least restrictive environment for these students.

EXAMPLES

- Have another student type for a student having difficulty typing an e-mail message, or type for this student yourself.

- Allow the student with special needs to view the slide show several times instead of completing the worksheet.

- Provide assistive technology devices to improve the functional capabilities of students with disabilities.

Instant Messaging

Objective

Students will exchange information with classmates using instant messaging (IM) and learn the meaning of 20 emoticons and acronyms.

Materials and Equipment

- paper and pencil for each student
- dry erase board and markers or chalkboard and chalk
- computer projection device
- Supplements 7F, 7G, 7H, 7I, 7J, 7K, 7L, 7M, and 7N

Supplement List

Below is a list of the lesson supplements that are on the accompanying CD, which is located in the back of this book. Use the CD to open the supplements and modify them, if desired.

SUPPLEMENT	TITLE	FORMAT
7F	Instant Messaging Resources	Word Document
7G	Instant Messaging Slide Show	PowerPoint Presentation
7H	Emoticon and Acronym Cards	Word Document
7I	Emoticons and Acronyms Slide Show	PowerPoint Presentation
7J	Instant Messaging Graph	Word Document
7K	Emoticons and Acronyms	Word Document
7L	Emoticons	Word Document
7M	Emoticons and Acronyms Answers	Word Document
7N	Emoticons Answers	Word Document

Procedures

Motivation

Strive to get students interested in IM, and then do your best to teach it to them. Choose an activity that engages and motivates them to learn.

EXAMPLES

- Write an emoticon on the board. Ask students to raise their hands and guess the meaning of the emoticon. For instance, :) means smile/happy, ;) denotes a wink.

- Say a few acronyms and ask if anyone in the class can explain its meaning. For instance, LOL means laughing out loud, and BTW stands for by the way. You could also come up with a fun sentence using as many acronyms as possible and write it on the board, or just say it to the class. Then say or write it again while giving the meaning of the acronyms.

- Ask students if anyone would like to share one fact that they already know about IM, allowing you to discover the prior knowledge base of the class.

- Do a simple drama to show that it is easy to focus entirely on sending and receiving instant messages, even for teachers.

- As students are entering the classroom, type on your computer and don't look up. Pretend that you are really involved in a heated IM discussion. As students wonder what you are doing and question when class is going to begin, tell students, "Just a minute, I'm instant messaging a friend right now." Then tell students that you were just acting like you were sending instant messages. Ask them, "Why is it important to realize what is going on around you?" Ask, "Have you ever seen anyone really involved in an IM discussion?"

Glossary Terms

acronym. A group of capital letters formed by using the first initial of a set of words.

emoticon. A symbol made using characters from the keyboard to express feelings online.

instant messaging. Messages that are electronically exchanged with another person in real time, often using nicknames.

Purpose

Be clear when explaining everything that the students will be doing in this lesson, so students know what is expected of them. Make this lesson meaningful by explaining the importance of knowing how to communicate using IM appropriately and ethically. Talk about ways that people actually use IM in a work environment, such as a school office communicating with classroom teachers at schools or nurses communicating with doctors at hospitals.

Instructional Input

Using IM is the focus for this part of the lesson. Communicate to students the specific information needed to IM as well as some background information. Add energy and enthusiasm while teaching so students will become intrigued and remember concepts more easily.

- Before class determine the method and become familiar with how you want the classes to send and receive IM. Use the Instant Messaging Resources (CD Supplement 7F) to create an instant messaging client for your class to send and receive IM.

- Project the Instant Messaging Slide Show (CD Supplement 7G) on the screen using the computer projector to expose students to instant messaging, emoticons, and acronyms, as well as to review Internet safety concepts from Unit 4, Digital Citizenship. One of the emoticons is for feeling "indifferent." Make sure that students understand this term.

- Write the glossary terms on the board and discuss their meaning with the class.

- Discuss and clearly show step-by-step how to send and receive IM using the computer connected to the projection device.

Sample Steps to Sending and Receiving IM

- Log in to your IM account.

- Click or type the screen name of the person you want to send a message to.

- Type a message and click "send" or press "enter."

- Watch for the person to send a message back to you.

Check for Understanding

The students should have a functional understanding of IM and how to send and receive messages. Determine whether students comprehend these concepts by watching for verbal and nonverbal clues. Consider all of your students' needs and adapt your teaching style to meet their learning needs when necessary.

- Have students say the steps or use the computer connected to the projector to show how to send and receive instant messages.

- Ask the students, "Why should you use proper behavior when typing instant messages?" Remind students that when you are talking to someone using IM, it is polite to continue the conversation. If you are unable to talk with the person, or if you need them to hold, then tell them to hold so they are not waiting too long.

- Ask the students, "How can you be safe when typing instant messages?" Here are a few examples:

  - Students should never give out personal information, including their screen name, when using IM because it is not secure and anyone can read it.

  - Students are responsible for the text that they type in any IM.

- Students should never meet with anyone or even talk to anyone they do not know when using IM.
- Ask students to explain the difference between an acronym and an emoticon.

Guided Practice

In this guided activity, students exchange information with classmates using IM. Think of the best way for each class to collaborate using instant messaging. Students will work in a planned manner to question and respond to classmates using IM to gather information.

EXAMPLES

- Distribute the Emoticon and Acronym Cards (CD Supplement 7H) to the class. Allow students to practice sending and receiving instant messages by talking with classmates on a given topic, such as: Internet safety, the benefits of using IM in the classroom, or the problems with students using IM. Students should write the particular acronym or emoticon on their card at least one time during the conversation. Here is a fun game to try!

    Step 1. Cut each card in half so that the emoticon is separate from its meaning and the acronym is separate from its meaning.

    Step 2. Pass out both parts of the cards to the class.

    Step 3. Have students send and receive IM to find out who has the match to their card, or have them walk around the room to find the match.

- Give the students a short article to read and then have students share their opinions about the article using IM.

Variations for Younger Students

This lesson will need to be modified to meet the needs of younger learners.

EXAMPLES

- Have students work with a partner to think about the meaning of the Emoticon and Acronym Cards (CD Supplement 7H).

    Step 1. Divide the class into groups of two or three students.

    Step 2. Pass out the cards.

    Step 3. Have students work with their partners to discuss the meaning of the card.

    Step 4. Ask each group to practice typing the emoticon or acronym on their computer.

    Step 5. Ask each group to share their card with the class. (Students could show the card, write it on the board, or type it into the computer connected to the projector.)

- Project the Emoticons and Acronyms Slide Show (CD Supplement 7I) on the class screen using the computer projector to expose students to 10 emoticons and 10 acronyms and their meanings. Show the slide show a second time and have students raise their hands or say the meaning together as a class as each emoticon and acronym appears on the screen.

- Allow students to send and receive messages as a class using the computer connected to the projector. Each student could be given a chance to come to the computer and type so that the students have an opportunity to use instant messaging. Here are a few suggestions of short, fun statements the students could type:

  - An emoticon

  - An acronym

  - Their favorite color, song, or sport

  - An answer to a question that you write on the board, such as "What do you want to be when you grow up?"

    - What they want to take to the moon: "I plan to travel in a space-ship to the moon, and I want to take _____."

- Have students type the emoticons using different word processors, showing that some word processors automatically change the emoticon into an actual smiley face, while other simple word processors, such as Notepad, keep the original characters they type.

Independent Practice

Think of the best way for each class to practice all that they have learned to make this information their own. You may decide to set a time limit so students stay focused on sharing the content.

EXAMPLES

- Have students send and receive IM to complete the Instant Messaging Graph (CD Supplement 7J) by asking at least five people if they prefer sending and receiving IM using a computer or text messaging using a cell phone.

- Ask students to send IM to inquire and gather information from classmates to complete the Emoticons and Acronyms worksheet (CD Supplement 7K) by writing the meaning of the emoticon or acronym in the space provided. Students could complete the Emoticons worksheet (CD Supplement 7L) by drawing a line from the emoticon to the correct face.

- Instruct students to write or type five ways a person can use IM appropriately and five ways he or she can use IM inappropriately.

- Have students write or type the meaning of instant messaging, acronym, and emoticon.

- Draw a few emoticons on the board and have students draw pictures of faces representing those emoticons. If students finish early, they could color the faces.

Assessment

Students have been given several opportunities to learn about instant messaging. Think of the best way for each class to be assessed at its particular learning level.

EXAMPLES

- Use the Emoticons and Acronyms Answers or Emoticons Answers (CD Supplement 7M or 7N) to check student work.

- Project the Emoticons and Acronyms Slide Show (CD Supplement 7I) on the class screen using the computer projector, and allow students to check their own work on the worksheets. Show the slide show a second time, and have students as a group say the meaning of the emoticon or acronym when it appears on the screen.

- Collect and assess the Instant Messaging Graph worksheets (CD Supplement 7J) for completeness.

- Have students share with the class some of their ideas on appropriate and inappropriate ways to use IM. Discuss the ramifications of using IM inappropriately.

- Choose various students to use the computer connected to the projector, and ask them to type a particular emoticon. Then have each student choose a classmate to share the meaning of the emoticon or acronym.

- Have students print out their IM conversations, and ask them to check for use of emoticons and acronyms while chatting.

Closure

Allow a few minutes for the students to reflect on all that they have learned about IM that day. This gives students a chance to process the information individually.

EXAMPLES

- Have students share one fact that they learned during the lesson.

- Ask students to share their screen names with the class.

- Encourage students to share the benefits or the possible problems of using IM in the classroom.

Extension

Consider the following extended activities to further the students' understanding of instant messaging.

EXAMPLES

- Have students create a pie chart on paper or on the computer using the information from the Instant Messaging Graph (CD Supplement 7J).

- Ask students to explain the similarities and differences between instant messaging and e-mail messages.

- Explain that many websites now offer online assistance using real people to send and receive IM to answer questions about products and services. Ask students to think about this IM concept and explain whether they think this assistance is helpful. Why or why not?

- Have students research the various IM clients used to send and receive IM and pick a favorite. Then have them write at least five reasons why it is their favorite and share them with the class.

- Design a lesson so that students have an opportunity to share files using IM to communicate with their peers.

- Have students explain how to mark that they are "away" or "offline" when using IM.

- Have a group brainstorming session using IM. Communicate with students using IM, allowing students to ask you questions or respond to you using IM. This gives opportunities for everyone, including shy students, to give input or pose questions. You could use the following questions: "What is the history of IM?" or "What is the future of IM?"

- Give students an opportunity to go online to search for more emoticons and acronyms and make a list of their favorites.

- Have students research how IM works using computers and servers and write a paragraph to be read to the class or given to the teacher.

- Write a contemporary topic on the board and tell students to discuss the topic with classmates using IM.

Remediation

Aim to meet the needs of any students who may need a little extra assistance. Be sensitive to these students, and think of new strategies to maximize their learning potential.

EXAMPLES

- Pair a student who needs extra assistance with another student who is willing to help.

- Have the student who needs help view the slide show at his/her seat again or at another time to reinforce instant messaging concepts.

- Allow the student to write instead of type any assignments that are given.

- Give the student extra opportunities to practice learning the emoticons and acronyms.

- Write out or print the steps to sending and receiving messages, and hang it on the wall so all students are able to see the steps while working.

Accommodation

Be sensitive to students with special needs or disabilities and make modifications to the lesson depending on individual needs. Consider the best ways to modify the lesson to provide the least restrictive environment for these students. There may be some students in your class with special needs who need a modified assignment or need to use instant messaging in a different way.

EXAMPLES

- Allow ample time for students to complete the worksheets, or only assign a section of the worksheet to students with exceptional needs.

- When using instant messaging, prepare these students' computers so that all they need to do is type a message instead of having to log on.

- Various assistive technology devices may be needed for these students to participate.

LESSON 3

VoIP and Videoconferencing

Objective

After a class discussion and teacher demonstration, students will communicate with other students using VoIP (Voice over Internet Protocol) and videoconferencing technologies to exchange information.

Materials and Equipment

- paper and pencil for each student
- dry erase board and markers or chalkboard and chalk
- camera or webcam
- VoIP phone and a regular telephone (optional)
- two pictures of a regular telephone (optional)
- globe or a picture of Earth (optional)
- large cardboard boxes (optional)
- computer projection device
- Supplements 7O, 7P, and 7Q

Supplement List

Below is a list of the lesson supplements that are on the accompanying CD, which is located in the back of this book. Use the CD to open the supplements and modify them, if desired.

SUPPLEMENT	TITLE	FORMAT
7O	VoIP and Videoconferencing Slide Show	PowerPoint Presentation
7P	Communications Graph (worksheet)	Word Document
7Q	VoIP and Videoconferencing	Word Document

Procedures

Motivation

Plan exciting classroom activities to get the students' attention focused on VoIP and videoconferencing.

EXAMPLES

- Use the VoIP and Videoconferencing Slide Show (CD Supplement 7O) to introduce students to VoIP and Videoconferencing concepts, as well as to review Internet safety concepts from Unit 4, Digital Citizenship.

- Before class set up a camera or webcam pointing to the students in the classroom, and display the live image onto the classroom screen using the computer connected to the projector. Tell students that today they will be learning about how to communicate on the Internet via a videoconference.

- Ask students to raise their hands if they have ever used VoIP or videoconferencing in the past. Have a few students share their experiences.

- Hold up a telephone and tell students that a telephone is no longer needed to make phone calls. Tell them there is a type of phone called VoIP (Voice over Internet Protocol).

- Hold up a VoIP phone and a regular phone and ask students to identify the similarities and differences between the two phones.

- Display a few different types of video cameras on the table in front of the classroom, and discuss the advantages of each camera when videoconferencing.

Purpose

To explain and show students the revolutionary idea of videoconferencing and making phone calls using the Internet.

Glossary Terms

videoconferencing. A real time video and audio communication over the Internet with two or more people in different locations.

VoIP. (Voice over Internet Protocol). A real time transmission of voice signals over the Internet.

Instructional Input

Think of simple, yet meaningful ways to convey the flexibility and convenience of using the Internet to make a phone call. Also, discuss with and show students how fun and easy it is to use videoconferencing. Explain the basics of how VoIP and videoconferencing work in various ways, adjusting to different classes' comprehension levels.

Note: Before this lesson, conduct a practice VoIP phone call and videoconference from your classroom to determine the best way to show these Internet messaging solutions to students. If you are unable to set up a VoIP or videoconference communication on the school's network, it may be blocked by the school's security network settings. Ask the network administrator to change the network security settings for this lesson. If the school does not allow this type of communication, be creative in showing students how it should work and explain why the school or county network blocks it.

EXAMPLES

- Write the glossary terms on the board and discuss their meanings with the class.

- Discuss how VoIP works by explaining the steps of making a phone call using the Internet. Show the class these steps on the screen using the computer connected to the projection device. More detailed steps may be added, depending on the way you want to make the VoIP call in your classroom.

Steps to making a VoIP Phone Call

1. Log onto a high speed Internet connection with VoIP software, such as Skype.

2. Decide which device you want to use to make a phone call over the Internet. There are three main ways to make a VoIP phone call.

   a. Use a computer with microphone and speakers

   b. Use a special VoIP phone

   c. Use a VoIP adapter with a regular telephone

3. Call and talk to a friend using his or her VoIP or regular phone line.

- Discuss how videoconferencing works by explaining the tools needed to make a videoconference. More detailed steps may be added depending on the way you want to videoconference in your classroom.

Tools Needed for a Videoconference

- Camera, webcam, or laptop with built in camera

- Speakers

- Microphone

- Monitor or projector

- Videoconferencing software or instant messaging software, such as Yahoo or Windows Live Messenger

- Internet connection

- Discuss a few of the advantages and disadvantages of using VoIP. A significant advantage is the ability to make free local and long distance calls to cell phones, other VoIP phones, and regular phones. A vital disadvantage is the need for electricity and a good Internet connection to make a clear phone call.

- Hang up two pictures of telephones with space between them on the board. Draw or hang up a picture of a globe in the middle of them.

Talk about how it is a revolutionary idea to talk on the phone using the Internet.

- Have three volunteers stand in front of the classroom to act out how a phone call is made using the Internet. Two students can be telephones, holding phones, while the student standing between them is the Internet. The student acting as the Internet could hold a globe or a picture of Earth. Whisper a message in the ear of one of the students acting as a phone. This student then whispers the message to the student standing as the Internet. Then, that student whispers the message to the other student acting as a telephone. Talk to the class about how the people are able to talk from one computer to another over the Internet.

- Discuss the possibility and advantages to communicating using a VoIP phone call and a videoconference simultaneously.

Check for Understanding

Determine the students' understanding of the lesson content by asking them questions in a fun way. Students could take turns standing in front of the live camera as they answer the question while the class watches them on the class screen connected to the projector.

EXAMPLES

- Ask the students, "What is VoIP? What is videoconferencing?"

- Have the students explain the importance of being safe and smart when using the Internet.

- Ask a student to explain how to make a VoIP phone call.

- Ask a student to explain how to communicate using videoconferencing.

- Have students explain the similarities and differences in telephone calls using POTS (plain old telephone system) and a telephone call using VoIP technology.

Guided Practice

Think of the best way for each class to practice making a VoIP phone call and having a videoconference. Observe students by walking around the room while they are working at their computers.

EXAMPLES

- Make a VoIP phone call and/or hold a videoconference with another classroom in your school, or in a different county, state, or country. The Internet can be a hazardous place, so research how to use student-friendly websites, such as ePals.com, to locate a school with similar interests. Communicate as a class to find out about the students in the other class.

- Allow various students to use the computer connected to the projector to show the steps in making a VoIP phone call as well as communicating using a videoconference. This activity will give students the opportunity to use VoIP and videoconferencing while allowing the class to see the steps.

Variations for Younger Students

Consider the following ways to modify this lesson to meet the needs of younger students.

EXAMPLES

- Set up a "pretend" VoIP and videoconferencing scenario. Use a regular telephone or cell phone and a live camera set up in the hall or another area so students cannot easily see the person in front of the camera.

- Record a video message discussing a popular topic, such as Internet safety, and show this video to students.

- Together as a class call the school principal using VoIP and discuss the importance of Internet safety.

- Bring in two large cardboard boxes and cut out the center of each one to make pretend monitors. Have students take turns standing behind the boxes and pretend to have a videoconference on certain topics. For example, the students could pretend to have a videoconference discussing the weather in different cities. Be creative and decorate the boxes in a fun manner.

Independent Practice

Depending on the grade level and technology available in your classroom, determine the best method for students to use this technology. Students could work as a class, in groups, with a partner, or individually.

EXAMPLES

- Have students communicate with another person in your classroom or another school using VoIP or videoconferencing and complete the Communications Graph worksheet (CD Supplement 7P). The graph shows the students' favorite ways to communicate, including talking in person, talking on the phone, sending e-mail messages, sending instant messages, or talking using video.

- Have students do research on the Internet to find three advantages and three disadvantages of using VoIP and videoconferencing and complete the VoIP and Videoconferencing worksheet (CD Supplement 7Q).

- Think of a creative way to assign partners, or have students pair up with the person sitting next to them in class. Have groups make a VoIP phone call to another group and/or communicate with them using videoconferencing within the classroom.

- Have students make VoIP phone calls while others use videoconferencing tools to find out specific information, and then ask them to write a paragraph explaining all they learned.

- Ask students to take turns communicating using the VoIP phone and/or videoconferencing with the computer connected to the class projector. Call upon different students to explain how to make a VoIP call or videoconference. When students give the correct step, have them go to the computer connected to the projector and perform the step for the class to see. Continue in this manner until everyone has a chance to go to the computer to complete a step.

- Have students write down on a piece of paper the steps of making a VoIP phone call or a videoconference.

- Instruct students to write down at least three Internet safety concepts to think about when communicating using the Internet.

Assessment

Consider one of the following assessments or design your own creative way to have students show their knowledge of this technology.

EXAMPLES

- Have students record the results of their graph on an enlarged graph for the entire class using the Communications Graph worksheet (CD Supplement 7P).

- Assign students or groups to give a presentation to the class on their research of the advantages and disadvantages of using VoIP and videoconferencing in the classroom using the VoIP and Videoconferencing worksheet (CD Supplement 7Q).

- Have students write or share the meanings of the terms discussed in this lesson, including VoIP and videoconferencing.

- As the students are working, observe and record each student's progress on a class roster or seating chart.

Closure

Allow students a few minutes to contemplate all that they have learned in the day's lesson on VoIP and videoconferencing.

EXAMPLES

- Have students share with a partner sitting next to them one thing that they learned about communicating via the Internet.

- Ask, "What have you learned today?"

- Allow students to write or draw a picture describing one thing they learned during the day's lesson.

Extension

Plan extended activities that will motivate students to continue to learn outside the classroom. Students could complete one of these for extra credit, or you may decide to include an activity for a class or homework assignment.

EXAMPLES

- Design an assignment that allows your class to communicate for a few months with another class in a different location using VoIP or videoconferencing. At a specific time, call another class and talk with them as a class, asking the students specific questions about their town. Allow that class to ask students in your class specific questions as well. Have students keep a journal with notes about the class and then discuss what they learned about the students.

- Ask how the military or a company ensures that video communications are secure when communicating secret information.

- If it is possible, set up morning announcements at your school using videoconferencing technology.

- Create an ongoing videoconference that could be used throughout the school during scheduled times. This will give students more opportunities to participate in a videoconference.

- Have students research the possibility for hackers to listen to a VoIP phone call.

- Challenge students to talk to their parents about using VoIP at home to place long-distance phone calls to relatives or friends.

- Have students research when the first videoconference was conducted.

- Have students research electronic communication using satellites in an interplanetary Internet and give a presentation to the class explaining how it works.

- Have students research the plethora of online classes that are now offered using videoconferencing and write a paragraph explaining how videoconferencing works with the online class.

Remediation

Consider one of the following examples to provide students with extra help needed to complete the lesson.

EXAMPLES

- Give the students a handout of detailed steps for making a VoIP phone call and setting up a videoconference.

- Pair students having difficulty with a partner who seems to understand the activity. Sometimes it helps to have one student explain the assignment to another student.

- Give students extra time when completing an activity to promote success among students.

Accommodation

Be sensitive to students with special needs or disabilities and make modifications to the lesson depending on individual needs. Consider the best ways to modify the lesson to provide the least restrictive environment for these students.

EXAMPLES

- Allow students with special needs to view the slide show several times to ensure that they have a chance to think about the information.

- Provide assistive technology devices to improve the functional capabilities of students with disabilities.

Multimedia Presentations

Unit Overview

This unit on Multimedia Presentations includes three lessons: Storyboarding, Multimedia Slide Shows, and Slide Show Presentations. This unit provides students with the opportunity to create an imaginative story and develop it into a multimedia slide show presentation. The Storyboarding lesson guides the students through writing a unique and creative story. Multimedia Slide Shows instructs the students in creating a slide show derived from the storyboard. The Slide Show Presentations lesson allows each student to share his or her presentation with an audience. At the completion of the Multimedia Presentations unit, students should be able to demonstrate the creation of a unique slide show presentation.

Unit Goal

To promote creative writing among students and encourage them to develop unique multimedia slide show presentations.

NETS•S Addressed

1. **Creativity and Innovation**

   Students demonstrate creative thinking, construct knowledge, and develop innovative products and processes using technology. Students:

   a. apply existing knowledge to generate new ideas, products, or processes

   b. create original works as a means of personal or group expression

   c. use models and simulations to explore complex systems and issues

   d. identify trends and forecast possibilities

Unit Variations for Younger Students

Students need confidence to be successful users of technology. You may want to alter the activities to meet the needs of each student more effectively. Reflect on the appropriate instruction method for younger students.

EXAMPLES

- Assign a story topic such as "counting" or "animals" to simplify the writing process for younger students.
- Require younger students to create fewer slides, depending upon their abilities.

Room Decorations

Students will be more excited about the topics if they look around and see changes in the learning environment. Consider ways to modify the computer lab to focus the students' attention on the unit's concepts.

- Dedicate a bulletin board or a section of the room to the slide show presentations. Print student slide show presentations and post them on a bulletin board in the room or in the hallway. Use a banner or letter cutouts to title the bulletin board "Slide Show Presentations."
- If you choose a topic for the stories, decorate the room using that theme, such as animals, seasons, holidays, poems, or sports.
- Change the desktop background to a screenshot of a popular children's book cover.
- Place several children's books on a table in the computer lab to refer to throughout the unit.

Storyboarding

Objective

After reading online stories, participating in a class discussion, and watching a teacher demonstration, students will write and illustrate an imaginative story on a storyboard.

Materials and Equipment

- pencil for each student
- dry erase board and markers or chalkboard and chalk
- children's storybooks or poems (optional)
- computer projection device
- Supplements 8A, 8B, 8C, and 8D

Supplement List

Below is a list of the lesson supplements that are on the accompanying CD, which is located in the back of this book. Use the CD to open the supplements and modify them, if desired.

SUPPLEMENT	TITLE	FORMAT
8A	Stories Online	Word Document
8B	Storyboard	Word Document
8C	Counting Storyboard	Word Document
8D	Storyboard Self-Assessment	Word Document

Procedures

Motivation

Incorporating a fun activity at the beginning of the lesson will generate students' interest and help them anticipate the upcoming material. Conceptualize an inspiring classroom environment for the motivating activity. This may be the first time students have viewed a story online, and the excitement will show on their faces.

- Motivate students by showing exciting stories from Stories Online (CD Supplement 8A) using the computer projector. The students could read the story together as a class, or you could read the story to them. Choose a student to advance the pages of the online story.

- Read or tell a fun and exciting familiar poem or story to the class.

Purpose

The lesson will acquire meaning for the students when they take ownership of the concepts and feel the lesson is worthwhile and important. Explain to students that they will read stories online to become familiar with the concepts and to encourage their own imaginations. Then they will develop a creative story using a storyboard. Students will become energized when they realize that their stories will be based on their original ideas. The lesson should be taught in a way that helps students to generate unique, thought-provoking ideas.

Instructional Input

In this part of the lesson, you will show students the way to read online stories. While the students are reading the online stories, encourage them to think about creative topics for their individual stories. Direct the students to websites that have stories geared toward their reading levels.

EXAMPLES

- Use the computer projector to show navigation techniques for the various websites listed on Stories Online (CD Supplement 8A).

- Choose various students to explain how to advance the pages of the online stories.

Check for Understanding

Students should have a clear understanding of the required tasks for this lesson. Check for comprehension by asking students to retell the lesson instructions. If the students do not seem to understand website navigation or the reason for reading the online stories, reteach the concepts again, using a different instruction technique.

EXAMPLES

- Ask questions concerning navigation through the websites to make certain the students grasp the concepts.

- Ask the students, "Why are you reading online stories?" Reinforce the point that students are reading online stories to inspire them to write individual stories.

Guided Practice

In this guided activity, students read the online stories. Carefully consider which approach will best motivate and inspire the students to put forth their best efforts.

EXAMPLES

- Have students begin reading selections from Stories Online (CD Supplement 8A) while pondering ideas for their own stories. Encourage students to share a favorite online story and the reason they liked the story. This may promote interest and attentiveness to possible writing ideas.

- Share some fun story ideas with the students, or ask questions to promote thoughts and stimulate original ideas.

- Encourage students to share their story ideas with the class to spark imagination and creativity throughout the class.

Variations for Younger Students

Modify the lesson to meet the individual needs of each student. Younger students may require more thought-provoking and inspirational ideas.

EXAMPLES

- Read one story together with the class, especially if the class is just learning to read.

- Read the story from the projector as the students read on their monitors at the same time.

- Tell an imaginative story about counting to motivate the students to think creatively.

Independent Practice

Allow time for students to begin writing. They may need to contemplate thoughts and ideas before starting to write. Clarify the number of pages the students will write on the storyboard, or allow the students to decide on the number of pages to include. Remind the students that the online stories may not be copied word for word because of copyright laws, nor may they copy the authors' ideas (plots).

EXAMPLES

- Explain to the students that the illustrations should be drawn in the box, and the corresponding sentences should be written on the lines using the Storyboard sheets with numbered boxes (CD Supplement 8B).

- If necessary, hold up a book and discuss a title page. Explain that the title of the book and the author's name appear on the cover of the book. Refer to the storyboard and explain that the title page is the same as the cover of a book.

Variations for Younger Students

Meet the needs of younger students while allowing them freedom in the writing process. Provide a different type of guidance for students requiring more help when writing. Take time to envision the best technique to guide the younger students in the class through the writing process.

EXAMPLES

- Allow younger students to create a counting story, entitled My Counting Story, using the Counting Storyboard (CD Supplement 8C). Have students write a word in the blank and draw the number of items corresponding to the number on the page. For example, the student may write "apples" on the blank and draw three apples.

- Ask a parent or another teacher to assist younger students in writing their storyboards.

- Write some words on the board or create a word bank to ensure correct spelling of frequently used words when the students begin writing. Have children's dictionaries available for students to use when writing the story.

Assessment

Decide upon the most appropriate means of assessment for the various classes. The assessment is an opportunity for students to shine and to share their ideas. Story alterations should be handled delicately to encourage the students at their own writing paces and levels.

EXAMPLES

- Have students edit their work using the Storyboard Self-Assessment (CD Supplement 8D).

- Instruct students to complete their individual stories on the storyboard. Evaluate them based on completion.

- Allow students to take their storyboards home to complete the story if extra time is needed. Evaluate the finished product.

- Check the papers for appropriateness and accuracy.

- Have students exchange papers with a partner to edit the work.

- Evaluate the students' stories for creativity and originality.

Closure

Think of a way to sum up the lesson effectively while encouraging the students in their efforts. Students will probably be satisfied with their efforts and the performance of their work if they know that they did their best. The students should feel proud of their accomplishments—writing their own stories.

- Remind students that they will be using their stories creating a slide show presentation during the next computer class.

- Encourage students to explain a few concepts they learned about writing a story.

Extension

Encourage students to go beyond the required assignment. When students become personally motivated, they will do all it takes to satisfy their desire to accomplish a goal.

- Submit a few well-written stories to a contest.

- Encourage students to write a sequel to their stories.

- Have students search the Internet for more online stories. This may result in the discovery of an interesting writing topic.

Remediation

Take into account the various levels of ability and understanding for this lesson. Students comprehend and write using many different styles and strategies. Modify the lesson to meet the needs of all students in the class.

- Incorporate writing strategies suitable for different types of learners.

- Provide students with poor writing skills extra assistance during or outside of class time.

- Allow more time for the students having difficulties to complete their stories.

- Share a prewritten storyboard with the class to reinforce the concept of writing a storyboard.

- If a student is having difficulty deciding upon a topic, ask the student questions to inspire creativity.

Accommodation

Be sensitive to students with special needs or disabilities and make modifications to the lesson depending on individual needs. Consider the best ways to modify the lesson to provide the least restrictive environment for these students.

EXAMPLES

- Allow students with special needs to read the online stories with a partner.
- Assign writing partners to students with special needs.
- Write the sentences on paper as the student with special needs speaks the story.
- Have students with disabilities draw the illustrations without sentences.
- Reduce the number of pages in the story for students with special needs.
- Provide assistive technology devices to accommodate students with disabilities.

LESSON 2

Multimedia Slide Shows

Objective

After a class discussion and teacher demonstration, students will design and produce a multimedia slide show presentation.

Materials and Equipment

- dry erase board and markers or chalkboard and chalk
- laser pointer (optional)
- floppy disks (optional)
- plastic comb (spiral) binding for each student (optional)
- slide show presentation software (see CD Supplement 8F)
- computer projection device
- Supplements 8B, 8C, 8E, 8F, 8G, and 8H

Supplement List

Below is a list of the lesson supplements that are on the accompanying CD, which is located in the back of this book. Use the CD to open the supplements and modify them, if desired.

SUPPLEMENT	TITLE	FORMAT
8B	Storyboard	Word Document
8C	Counting Storyboard	Word Document
8E	My Counting Story Sample	PowerPoint Presentation
8F	Multimedia Slide Show Help	Word Document
8G	Slide Show Template	PowerPoint Presentation
8H	My Counting Story Template	PowerPoint Presentation

Procedures

Motivation

The opening activity should focus the students' attention on creating a slide show and generating new ideas on animating their individual stories.

EXAMPLES

- Motivate the students by showing the My Counting Story Sample (CD Supplement 8E), using the computer connected to the projector.

- Encourage students to imagine that each of their stories is being turned into a movie. The students could think about and discuss the various scenes in their movies (characters, backgrounds, colors, and themes).

Purpose

This lesson integrates creative writing with technology. The students' concepts will be taken from basic ideas to beautiful animated slide show presentations. Explain that the students will be using their stories to design multimedia slide show presentations to present to the class.

Instructional Input

At this point you will model the steps to creating a slide show using a simple, step-by-step demonstration. The students' previous experiences with slide shows will determine the level of instruction necessary. It may be a challenge to produce clear, practical steps for a variety of levels and learning styles.

EXAMPLES

- Refer to the Multimedia Slide Show Help document (CD Supplement 8F) for information on creating a slide show presentation.

- To create their presentation, have students refer to their stories written on the Storyboard or Counting Storyboard (CD Supplements 8B and 8C).

- Using the computer projector, model the following steps to create a slide show. Show the students the process one step at a time, and then give them a couple of minutes to complete the step before showing them the next procedure. Have students sit with their hands in their laps when you are explaining the steps. This will ensure that the students hear and see all the steps.

  Step 1. Open a template or create a new presentation. Direct the students to open the Slide Show Template (CD Supplement 8G) from a shared folder or create a new presentation at their computer workstations. If a shared folder is used, students could open the template and then save their slide shows in a specified subfolder. Have them save a backup copy to a floppy disk or another portable storage device.

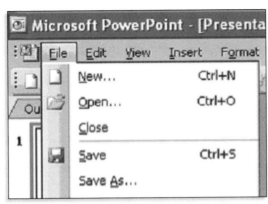

FIGURE 3. Creating a new presentation using Microsoft PowerPoint.

FIGURE 4. Creating a new presentation using Impress Presentation.

Step 2. Create a title page. Have the students create the title page using the storyboard. It should include the title and the author's name. A graphic is optional.

Step 3. Type sentences. Instruct the students to type all the sentences in the storyboard using text or word art. The students should consider the font size and style to create a story that flows when reading.

Step 4. Insert graphics. Direct the students to insert graphics to illustrate each page. The graphics should flow to create a meaningful story. For example, if a student has written a story about a bird learning to fly, each page should have a graphic with the same type of bird. Show the students the process of going on the Internet to locate a certain graphic. The pages should look well proportioned, and the pictures should fill up the entire page. Show some pages of a book to illustrate this point.

Step 5. Include multimedia effects (animations, transitions, sounds, and backgrounds). Instruct the students to animate at least one graphic or text on each slide. If needed, develop guidelines for the amount and type of multimedia elements added to the presentation. The students may ask another student to read their sentences and look at their graphics for accuracy before adding multimedia effects to the presentation.

Variations for Younger Students

Carefully monitor the countenance of younger students to determine their levels of understanding. Teach the steps at a pace that promotes achievement for all students.

EXAMPLES

- It may be easier for younger students to open and use the My Counting Story Template (CD Supplement 8H). If the Counting Storyboard was used in Lesson 1, then the My Counting Story Template will complement this template.

- It may be easier for younger students to type the words and insert the graphics for each slide at the same time instead of typing all of the words first.

- You may have to teach the steps several times and have younger students repeat them to ensure comprehension.

- You may choose to teach each step separately and have the younger students complete steps one at a time, rather than teaching all the steps at once.

- Students could choose one graphic for the entire story. Explain how to copy and paste that graphic onto the other slides. You may need to discuss that one graphic is on the first page and two graphics are on the second page; then continue in this manner to page 5, the last page.

Check for Understanding

By this point, the students should feel confident about creating a slide show. They should be familiar with all the steps and understand the flow of the process from step to step. Strive to involve as many students as possible when checking for under-standing to determine the comprehension level of the entire class. If the students do not seem to understand the steps of creating a slide show, you may need to teach a specific step or steps again.

EXAMPLES

- Have students briefly restate the instructions, or steps, for creating a slide show presentation.

- Ask questions about which item to click on to do a specific task. Have a student use the laser pointer to point to the screen and show the class.

Guided Practice

Ask the students to model the steps for creating a slide show. Some students may feel challenged during this activity; monitor the anxiety levels of students. Encourage students to be clear and concise when sharing the steps with the class. Allowing the students to teach will develop their confidence and train them to demonstrate effective communication skills. Help the students during the demonstrations, if needed. Each student should feel engaged in this lesson; therefore, be sensitive to keeping the learning environment relaxed and supportive. When deciding upon the level of instruction, always consider the various ability levels of the students.

- Have the students take turns using the computer connected to the projector to demonstrate the steps for completing a slide show on the class screen.

- Have two students work together to explain the steps for creating a slide show. One student could explain the steps needed to complete a slide, while the other moves the mouse using the computer projector.

- Tell students there is more than one way to complete the steps in this lesson. If students know a shortcut or a different way to complete a step, let them demonstrate using the computer connected to the projector.

Independent Practice

During this independent practice, students create their own slide shows. Most students will be delighted to create their own presentations. The creativity and self-expression inherent in the lesson will inspire most students to put forth their best work. Students should begin with the "end" in mind, which may help them overcome obstacles while working. This means that students should decide on a goal and then figure out the way to get there. Direct students to complete Steps 1 through 5, listed previously under Instructional Input, to create their slide show presentations.

EXAMPLES

- Have students use Microsoft PowerPoint (see Fig. 7) or Open Office (see Fig. 8, Impress Presentation) to create their multimedia presentations. If necessary, refer to Multimedia Slide Show Help (CD Supplement 8F).

- Write the steps for creating a slide show on the board, for easy reference.

Assessment

In this lesson, students have had several opportunities to display their abilities while developing their slides. Decide which evaluation methods will best reveal each class's accomplishments. Take into consideration the various abilities and environmental factors (such as technical difficulties) when grading the students.

Give students ample opportunities to excel through a variety of means. Students will work hard by nature because they will want to achieve satisfaction in developing a fantastic slide show.

- Observe and record participation as the students create a slide show presentation and demonstrate the steps for creating a slide show.

- Observe students to determine whether they are following the correct steps when creating the slides.

- Have students print their slide show presentations for evaluation when they are complete.

Closure

The students will find fulfillment in knowing their slide show presentations are complete. Commend the students for their achievements in a creative manner. Think about a way to close this lesson with encouragement and praise for all the work accomplished.

EXAMPLES

- Remind the students that they will share their slide show presentations during the next computer class.

- Have students explain one fact learned when creating a slide show.

- Invite students to encourage each other on their slide shows to ensure that all students are supported in their efforts.

Extension

The excitement and style of the lesson may motivate students to want to create a variety of slide show presentations. Think of additional ideas to expand the horizon of students who want to do more.

EXAMPLES

- Encourage students to complete a tutorial on the presentation software, using a website from the Multimedia Slide Show Help (CD Supplement 8F).

- Print, cut, and make the slides into books using comb binding. Distribute these books to the students on the day of the slide show presentations. Students may color these books and read them to a friend.

- Have students create an additional slide show just for fun with few or no guidelines. This gives them a chance to be creative and attempt new procedures. One suggestion is for students to create a presentation describing themselves or their families.

- If students complete their presentations early, allow them to explore the presentation software for other options, such as music, sounds, background colors, additional graphics, and more animation.

Remediation

During the lesson, be aware of students who are getting behind and off track. These students may require extra assistance when working on their slide shows. If students appear to be behind, you may need to teach a section of the lesson again to part of the class. Think about the best way to teach the material again in a different way to the students who need extra help.

EXAMPLES

- To give students time to absorb the material, teach this lesson in two days.

- Write out and distribute the five steps for students to follow more closely.

- Allow students to help students sitting next to them when working on the slide show independently. Students finishing their slide shows early may help the students requiring assistance.

- Have one student create his or her presentation using the computer connected to the computer projector. In this way, other students will be able to see how the steps for creating a slide show are accomplished while the student is demonstrating each one.

Accommodation

Be sensitive to students with special needs or disabilities and make modifications to the lesson depending on individual needs. Consider the best ways to modify the lesson to provide the least restrictive environment for these students. If a student is noticeably behind when creating the slide show, talk privately with this student. Set up a plan to accommodate a work load that doesn't overwhelm the student and dampen the excitement.

EXAMPLES

- Allow students with special needs to work with a partner to complete the slide show presentation.

- Type the sentences or provide other assistance for students with special needs.

- Require students with disabilities to complete only some of the slides.

- Select a specific font size and style for the template, making it easier for students with special needs to succeed in this lesson.

- Use any assistive technology devices needed for these students to create their presentations.

Slide Show Presentations

Objective

Students will rehearse and present their multimedia slide shows to the class using the appropriate presentation techniques.

Materials and Equipment

- pencil for each student
- each student's saved slide show presentation
- computer projection device
- Supplements 8I and 8J

Supplement List

Below is a list of the lesson supplements that are on the accompanying CD, which is located in the back of this book. Use the CD to open the supplements and modify them, if desired.

SUPPLEMENT	TITLE	FORMAT
8I	Slide Show Assessment	Word Document
8J	Multimedia Record	Word Document

Procedures

Motivation

Plan an activity to spark students' enthusiasm for the class presentations.

EXAMPLES

- Create a fun slide show presentation to share with the class.
- Share a personal experience about the sense of accomplishment you felt when you completed a project.

Purpose

The purpose of the lesson is to give students the opportunity to present their work to the class and respond to the work of others. This may be the students' first formal class presentation using technology. Explain that students will read their slide show presentations to the class, using correct presentation practices as the class respectfully watches and listens. Each student will present his or her own story using the computer projector.

Instructional Input

At this point you will want to discuss slide show presentation techniques. When deciding the method for teaching presentation practices, consider the variety of learning styles. The students should feel secure when sharing their stories. This is a time for students to stand out and show their personalities. This assignment may be remembered for the student's entire life. The atmosphere should be accepting and nonthreatening, allowing everyone to feel self-assured.

EXAMPLES

- Discuss the requirements on the Slide Show Assessment (CD Supplement 8I) so that students will become aware of the evaluation criteria.

- Explain that students will come to the projector one at a time to share their slide show presentations.

- Review the following presentation practices before beginning the presentations.
    1. Speak in a clear, strong voice.
    2. Be lively when you read.
    3. Practice reading your story.
    4. Stand up straight.
    5. Be confident.
    6. Be familiar with the way to navigate your slide show. (Explain the term "navigate.")

Check for Understanding

Make certain that the students understand your expectations for the presentations. Think of a creative way to ensure that the students know the important concepts. If the students do not seem to understand the process for correctly and appropriately presenting their slide show, you may need to demonstrate the instructions again.

EXAMPLES

- Have students restate the procedures for presenting the slide shows to the class.

- Ask students to explain the proper presentation practices.

Guided Practice

In this guided practice, students rehearse their slide show presentations. Share your enthusiasm with the students and watch the excitement spread as students anticipate presenting their stories to the class. Give students the opportunity to rehearse their slides with a partner. Practicing with a partner should help students feel more assured.

EXAMPLES

- Give students printouts of the Slide Show Assessment (CD Supplement 8I) so that they can read the evaluation criteria. Have students write their names on the sheet and turn it in when it is their turn to present.

- Have students practice reading their stories with a partner in slide show layout. This practice generates confidence in the students. Here are some steps for this technique.

    1. Choose the partners or let the students choose partners.

    2. Have students take turns practicing their presentations with a partner at their individual computers.

    3. Make sure students know the way to navigate correctly during the slide show presentation. Offer assistance when necessary.

Glossary Terms

multimedia. The integration of text, graphics, sound, and animation using a computer.

navigate. To move the slide presentation from slide to slide using the mouse.

Independent Practice

This is the pinnacle of the Multimedia Presentations unit; the students will share their slide show stories with the class. Create an accepting atmosphere so that students will feel comfortable when sharing. Even though students may be nervous about sharing their stories, once they have completed their presentations, they should feel a sense of achievement. The class should listen politely and intently as the slide shows are presented. Review manners and appropriate behavior before the presentations begin. During the presentations, it will be interesting to see the personality of each student presenter portrayed in the story and multimedia effects.

EXAMPLES

- Have the audience look for interesting multimedia elements in the presentations to complete the Multimedia Record (CD Supplement 8J).

- Instruct students to share their stories with the audience using the computer projector. Take volunteers by asking the students to raise their hands to present, or call on students randomly or in alphabetical order to present their slide shows.

Variations for Younger Students

Carefully consider which approach will provide the best environment for all students. Strive to motivate the students to feel confident in their approach to the presentations.

EXAMPLES

- Open the presentation and transition from one slide to the next for the younger students.
- Read the story to the class or have the students read the words aloud as a class.

Assessment

The lesson could be assessed in a variety of ways. Think about the best way to assess each class accurately, taking into account the various learning styles and abilities. Throughout the lesson, give the students many opportunities to succeed and shine individually.

EXAMPLES

- Assess the students on specific requirements using the Slide Show Assessment sheet (CD Supplement 8I).
- Collect the Multimedia Record (CD Supplement 8J) and grade it for completeness.
- Take note of whether each student completed and presented a slide show story to the class.
- Observe the audience during the presentations and evaluate their behavior. Question students on the presentations to determine how well they were listening.
- Note whether students encouraged one another when reviewing the presentations.
- Grade students on how well they were able to navigate their slides.
- Observe student participation during class discussions.

Closure

Students should feel a sense of accomplishment at the completion of the multimedia slide show presentations. Praise them for having succeeded with such a big task. Think about an appropriate way to end this lesson while commending the students for a job well done and challenging them to set even higher goals.

EXAMPLES

- Encourage students to share the results from the Multimedia Record (CD Supplement 8J).

- Commend the students on successful completion of a multimedia project that integrated creative writing with technology.

- Have students share some of the good ideas used in the presentations including animations, storylines, and graphics.

- Ask students to write a letter to a person in the class that talks about what they liked about the individual's multimedia story.

- Pass out certificates for the best presentations or for all the presentations.

Extension

This lesson is likely to spark the creativity of many students. Think of fun and innovative ways to kindle that flame with lesson extensions. Various ideas for challenging and motivating students are offered in the following list.

EXAMPLES

- If the books were created using comb binding, have students read the books to a classmate. Encourage students to color their books and bring them back to class for extra credit.

- Pass out paper and pencils before or after the presentations for the students to write down excellent ideas seen during the presentations.

- If there is time, have students watch presentations from other classes.

- Combine all the student slide shows into one class presentation to be shown at one time.

- Invite parents, teachers, and administrators to see the students' slide show presentations. This is a great opportunity for parents and administrators to see all that the students are learning in the computer lab!

- For homework or extra credit, have students color or decorate their books and bring them back to class.

Remediation

Repeat a section of the lesson if necessary. During class, monitor students' responses and body language for comprehension of the concepts being taught.

EXAMPLES

- Give the students ample time to review their slide shows before presenting.

- Allow students having difficulty to present to you before presenting to the entire class.
- If students are struggling during the slide show rehearsals, assist them with their presentations.

Accommodation

Be sensitive to students with special needs or disabilities and make modifications to the lesson depending on individual needs. Consider the best ways to modify the lesson to provide the least restrictive environment for these students.

The following examples may provide assistance in accommodating students with special needs.

EXAMPLES

- If a student with special needs does not understand the process for sharing the slide show, have another student assist him or her in giving the presentation.
- You may wish to view the presentation without a class audience, depending upon the individual needs of the student.

Online Learning

Unit Overview

This unit entitled Online Learning includes two lessons: Virtual Field Trips and Online Encyclopedias. In the first lesson, Virtual Field Trips, students work cooperatively and go online to conduct research, record findings, and present the information to the class. In the Online Encyclopedias lesson, students work collaboratively to solve problems by gathering data and investigating solutions. This unit will instruct students in online learning techniques while teaching them to form opinions based on research.

Unit Goal

To allow students to work in cooperative groups to conduct research, process information, and present findings to the class.

NETS•S Addressed

4. **Critical Thinking, Problem Solving, and Decision Making**

Students use critical thinking skills to plan and conduct research, manage projects, solve problems, and make informed decisions using appropriate digital tools and resources. Students:

   a. identify and define authentic problems and significant questions for investigation

   b. plan and manage activities to develop a solution or complete a project

   c. collect and analyze data to identify solutions and/or make informed decisions

   d. use multiple processes and diverse perspectives to explore alternative solutions

Unit Variations for Younger Students

Contemplate the best way to impart online learning techniques to younger students, including research methods and cooperative work. As younger students are working, modify and simplify the lessons in fun and creative ways to meet the needs of the class.

EXAMPLES

- Choose one or two sites from the Virtual Field Trip Websites (CD Supplement 9A) and the Encyclopedia Websites (CD Supplement 9G). This will lead to more successful research because students will be more focused.

- Choose and focus on a primary theme, such as farm animals, planets, ocean animals, habitats, dinosaurs, or the continents, to excite the students and motivate them to learn. The example on CD Supplement 9B is the solar system.

- Have students complete the research as a class and discuss the information they found on the Internet.

- Focus on one or two planets or other space objects throughout the unit.

- Instead of focusing on the research portions of the lessons, have younger students collect and analyze information by looking at pictures and watching videos.

Room Decorations

Think of a way to decorate the computer lab to excite the students about the solar system. The materials used to enhance the room could be referred to throughout the unit. The solar system decorations do not need to be large and difficult to create; just a simple room rearrangement or a fun manipulative could change the atmosphere and motivate the students. Be inventive.

EXAMPLES

- Print and display the solar system pictures from the Solar System Slide Show (CD Supplement 9B). *Note:* Before printing, change the color of the background to white so that it does not use all of the black ink in your printer. Just right-click on the slide and choose "background" to change the color.

- If a theme is implemented for this unit, for example, the solar system, the human body, the ocean, or seasons, decorate the room with posters and other creative items related to the theme.

- Hang glow-in-the-dark stars and planets around the room.

- Create letter cutouts or a banner to designate an area of the room as the "Online Learning" bulletin board. Hang pictures of the solar system, stars, planets, comets, and other planetary objects.

- Imaginatively display pictures of various objects in the solar system around the room.

- Change the desktop background of the lab computers to a picture of the solar system or another planetary object to represent the solar system theme.

- Build a spaceship or rocket out of a large cardboard box (e.g., a refrigerator box) and allow students to take turns going into the spaceship.

Note: The supplements, websites, and examples for this unit are based on the solar system; however, the theme may be modified to suit your needs.

LESSON 1

Virtual Field Trips

Objective

After a class discussion, students will work collaboratively to conduct research about the solar system using virtual field trips on the Internet and then present their findings to the class.

Materials and Equipment

- paper and pencil for each student
- dry erase board and markers or chalkboard and chalk
- star stickers (optional)
- computer projection device
- Supplements 9A, 9B, 9C, 9D, 9E, and 9F

Supplement List

Below is a list of the lesson supplements that are on the accompanying CD, which is located in the back of this book. Use the CD to open the supplements and modify them, if desired.

SUPPLEMENT	TITLE	FORMAT
9A	Virtual Field Trip Websites	Word Document
9B	Solar System Slide Show	PowerPoint Presentation
9C	Solar System Topics	Word Document
9D	Fact Gathering I	Word Document
9E	Fact Gathering II	Word Document
9F	Group Assessment	Word Document

Procedures

Motivation

Ignite your students' enthusiasm with an exciting opening activity. In this lesson students will take a virtual field trip to the solar system. One of these motivating activities could be used to focus the students' attention toward online learning.

EXAMPLES

- Project an exciting video or picture on the class screen with the computer projector using a website from the Virtual Field Trip Websites (CD Supplement 9A). Have students discuss the video or picture with the class.

- Project the Solar System Slide Show (CD Supplement 9B) onto the class screen using the computer connected to the projector. Allow students to say the various solar system objects as they appear on the screen.

- Write this quote on the board or play a sound clip of Neil Armstrong's first words on the moon: "That's one small step for a man, one giant leap for mankind." Talk to the students about what this sentence means.

- Ask the class if they have ever seen a space shuttle blast off into outer space or if they have ever seen a shooting star. The students could share some personal experiences.

- Ask students to write down as many solar system terms as they can think of in one minute. This allows you to see the students' prior knowledge.

- Make a space suit or obtain a space suit costume and wear it during the lesson.

- To motivate students tell them that you will give out stickers at the end of the class to students who are participating and listening throughout the lesson. You could use small star stickers to continue the solar system theme. You could even give a special prize to a student who listens and participates well throughout the lesson.

- Tell the students that they will be going on a class field trip today, but there is no need to bring field trip money or a sack lunch because the field trip will be a virtual field trip.

- For fun have students type and then share the things that they would like to take with them on an imaginary field trip to outer space.

Purpose

This lesson allows students to take a field trip into outer space, a place that some of them might actually be able to visit one day. Thinking about taking a field trip into space may excite the students. Tell students that they will be working in groups to do research and then sharing this information with the class.

> **Glossary Term**
>
> **virtual field trip.** A visit to websites to learn about a particular topic through unique online experiences.

Instructional Input

Design a lesson that will bring students to new understandings of online learning using virtual field trips. Think of the best way to demonstrate how the virtual field trip works for each class level.

EXAMPLES

- Choose a virtual field trip from the Virtual Field Trip Websites (CD Supplement 9A) to show students how it works. A student could use the computer connected to the projector to show the class on the screen the steps to opening the website as you read the steps to the class.

- Write the steps to using the virtual field trip website on the board for students to refer to throughout the lesson if needed.

- Write the term "virtual field trip" on the board and discuss the meaning with the class.

Check for Understanding

Students should feel comfortable when going online to the virtual field trip website. Be imaginative when asking the students to retell the steps for using the field trip websites and finding information on the solar system. Think of ways to provide positive reinforcement to the students when determining their comprehension levels. If the students do not seem to understand the steps for using the website, you may need to teach the lesson again using a different method.

EXAMPLES

- Ask, "What is unique about a virtual field trip?"

- Have students retell the steps of how to go online to the virtual field trip website to ensure that they understand. Give them a sticker or praise for their efforts.

- Ask a volunteer to explain how to open and navigate the virtual field trip website while another student uses the computer connected to the projector to show these steps.

- Ask some questions about what is expected of them, and have each student in the class give thumbs up for "yes" and thumbs down for "no." This will allow you to see if anyone doesn't understand.

Guided Practice

Contemplate creative ways to assign groups and topics, and provide students with the information needed to begin their group projects. Try to get them excited about completing this assignment. The solar system is an intriguing subject because there is so much we do not know about it. If students sense your excitement and desire to learn more about the solar system, they will become excited, too. If needed, allow students with special needs to practice using the virtual field trip with your guidance so they will feel comfortable with online learning within the group.

EXAMPLES

- Here is a fun way to assign topics:

    1. Print out and hang the pictures of solar system objects using the Solar System Slide Show images (CD Supplement 9B). Hang the pictures from the ceiling all around the room using string. Be sure to hang them above the computers or students' chairs. If you are unable to hang the pictures, you could tape a picture to each row of computers, certain chairs, or another location in your room. *Note:* Before printing, change the color of the background to white so that it does not use all of the black ink from your printer. Just right-click on the slide's black background and choose the slide background command to change the color.

    2. Place the students in groups according to their abilities. Try to make the performance within each group as equivalent as possible. Depending upon the class and grade levels, it may be beneficial to give each student a card with a specific task on it, such as leader, time manager, researcher, writer, illustrator, or presenter. Students could be given more than one task within each group. Provide clear guidelines for each job.

    3. After the groups have been assigned, tell each group to look up to the solar system object hanging above their computer or to find the solar system picture closest to their group's location. Explain that this object is their solar system topic to research using the virtual field trip.

- Use the Solar System Topics (CD Supplement 9C) to assign topics. Print and cut out the solar system objects from the list and give one to each group.

- The groups could be assigned based on students' or each group's interest in a certain solar system topic.

- Give students a sample solar system object, such as the Sun, and have them use the virtual field trip websites to locate a fact about it. Ask a few students to share their facts with the class and tell how they found it. Ask another student to come to the board and draw a picture of the object after viewing it online.

Variations for Younger Students

The younger students will probably need more guidance. Plan ways to give students as much freedom as possible while allowing them to experience the virtual field trip at their own levels. Consider modifying the lesson for these beginning learners.

EXAMPLES

- Display a website on the class screen using the computer projector, and discuss the procedures for navigating and finding information on the site, such as looking for pictures, boldfaced words, and hyperlinks. For younger students, choose only one or two websites from the Virtual Field Trip Websites (CD Supplement 9A).

- Show students the virtual field trip website using your computer, and have students click exactly where you click on their individual computers. Have them sit with their hands folded while you click a few links, and then allow them to click until they arrive at the same page. Continue in this manner so that students learn how to navigate the site.

- Have the entire class study and draw a picture of one or a few solar system objects.

- Instead of assigning jobs for every person in the group, just assign one job per group, such as group leader.

Independent Practice

Explain that students will be responsible for their efforts within the group. Students work with group members to go to the virtual field trips' websites and record information on their fact gathering worksheets (printed out from CD Supplements 9D and 9E). Students work together so that the group becomes an expert on the topic.

Establish boundaries and requirements before the students begin to work. This will keep them focused on their project and help them understand all that is expected of them. Ensure that each student is given a specific task. Encourage group members to assist each other and provide feedback within the group. Some students may have more than one task.

EXAMPLES

- Have groups work with group members to complete the Fact Gathering I or II worksheet (CD Supplements 9D or 9E), where they will list facts and draw a picture of the solar system object. You could distribute one worksheet per group or require each student to complete a worksheet.

- Talk to the class about ways the group can work together to strengthen their efforts. You may decide to discuss a few group rules. Here are some rules you may want to use:

    1. Help and encourage other group members.

    2. Stay on task.

    3. Talk quietly.

    4. Complete your work.

    5. Make sure every member of the group participates.

Assessment

Determine the best way to measure students' achievements concerning online learning using virtual field trips during this lesson. Think of ways to assess the manner in which individuals participated collaboratively within the group.

- Each student completes a Group Assessment form (CD Supplement 9F) showing the efforts of the other group members. This form could be used as part of their grade for this lesson.

- Groups share information with the class about their solar system topic. The groups could choose one group member to share, or each person could share one fact. Another option is to designate a reporter who is assigned to record and present the group's findings.

Closure

Recap the purposes of the lesson, and give the students a few minutes to contemplate all that they have learned. Students should understand that this lesson was a meaningful activity both because of the information they learned about the solar system and because they learned how to work together in groups. Encourage students to relate the virtual field trip to an actual field trip.

EXAMPLES

- Encourage students to share some of the interesting facts they learned about the solar system.

- Have students share some advantages of a virtual field trip.

- Ask students to explain the importance of knowing online research techniques and locating trustworthy sources of information.

- Point to any solar system object located in the classroom, and have students say the name of the object.

- Ask students to share one positive trait of a person in their group. Have students share how working with others helped them during the lesson.

Extension

This virtual field trip lesson on the solar system may have excited students concerning the solar system and virtual field trip websites. The following ideas may be used to extend their understanding.

EXAMPLES

- Take an actual field trip to a local planetarium or science museum.

- Have students conduct research about the latest space exploration and share the information with the class.

- Have groups create slide show presentations on their solar system topics and share them with the class.

- Have students work in their groups to research a topic in more depth and present to the class a research paper with an outline and note cards. Students could create a diagram using poster board or make models of their space objects.

Remediation

Throughout the lesson, monitor students as they are working. If you sense that a student needs extra assistance, try to help the student at that time or at the first appropriate opportunity.

EXAMPLES

- Arrange groups so that students are placed according to ability to ensure each group has about the same performance level. This may mean placing good readers with poor readers or nonreaders.

- Work with a student who is behind during independent practice to fill in any information gaps.

- Ask a student having difficulties questions to promote individual thinking, such as, "What do you think you should do next?"

Accommodation

Be sensitive to students with special needs or disabilities and make modifications to the lesson depending on individual needs. Consider the best ways to modify the lesson to provide the least restrictive environment for these students. The following examples are some suggestions on how to modify your lesson.

EXAMPLES

- Require students with special needs to complete only some of the information on the Fact Gathering I or II worksheet (CD Supplements 9D or 9E).

- Have a resource or special education teacher assist these students with the activity using one-to-one instruction.

- Have the website already open on these students' computers, or allow another student to help.

- Allow students with special needs to work independently instead of in a group.

LESSON 2

Online Encyclopedias

Objective

After a collaborative group effort to collect and analyze data using online encyclopedias, students will answer questions and solve real-world problems.

Materials and Equipment

- paper and pencil for each student
- dry erase board and markers or chalkboard and chalk
- set of encyclopedias (optional)
- computer projection device
- Supplements 9F, 9G, 9H, and 9I

Supplement List

Below is a list of the lesson supplements that are on the accompanying CD, which is located in the back of this book. Use the CD to open the supplements and modify them, if desired.

SUPPLEMENT	TITLE	FORMAT
9F	Group Assessment	Word Document
9G	Encyclopedia Websites	Word Document
9H	Solar System Questions	Word Document
9I	Postcard Template	Word Document

Procedures

Motivation

An exciting activity will set the tone for this lesson and generate enthusiasm. Think of an event that will motivate and inspire the students to listen and learn. This lesson is geared toward the free thinkers and innovative students, so if a student likes to be told exactly what to do, this project-based learning activity will be a great opportunity for him or her to experience a new type of learning. This activity will get the students to think about the project they will do in class.

EXAMPLES

- Bring in a set of encyclopedias and place them somewhere in the computer lab so that students can see them. Explain that they will be researching using encyclopedias, but not the hard copies sitting in the computer lab; students will be using online encyclopedias.

- Hold up an encyclopedia. Show students how to look up information on Mars in an actual encyclopedia. Then show them the encyclopedia online and talk about the similarities and differences between the two methods of collecting information.

- Sing *Twinkle, Twinkle, Little Star* or another song about space to get the students thinking about space.

- Using the computer projector, show a video of a problem in the world, such as pollution, overpopulation, or other environmental issues. Encourage the class to discuss this problem and possible solutions.

- Have students share several real-world problems and talk about their feelings.

- Complete an activity that allows the students to determine and think about their individual learning styles. This may help students realize how they learn best as well as indicate to them which learning styles to improve while working.

    1. Have students watch a video that gives verbal facts about space. This should last about two minutes, so you may need to show only part of the video. Some suggestions are the DVDs from the Magic School Bus Space Adventures (www.scholastic.com/magicschoolbus/tv/episodes/space_adventures.htm) or some online videos from NASA (www.nasa.gov/multimedia/videogallery/Video_Archives_Collection_archive_1.html).

    2. Give the students five minutes to write down some facts that they learned from the video.

    3. Watch the video again and direct the students to circle the facts that were learned from the pictures and put a star next to the facts that were learned from the verbal facts (words).

    4. If the student circles more facts, he or she may be a visual learner. If the student places a star next to more facts, the student may be an auditory learner.

Purpose

In today's Information Age, information really is at our fingertips. Students can use a search engine or an online encyclopedia to search for answers to questions and find out more about a subject. During this lesson, students will become familiar with how to use online encyclopedias as well as understand the importance of credible sources. This lesson provides students with an opportunity to solve a real-world problem while working collaboratively. After the students have been given the opportunity to search for information on a world problem, the lesson will end with student presentations of their research and solutions. This is an authentic learning experience based on team research and reflection.

Instructional Input

Carefully determine the type of activity to assign
each class. You might have students continue
with the solar system or a related theme now that
students have a background in the topic from the
previous lesson. Students should be involved in all
aspects of the project including choosing a topic,
organizing research, and presenting their findings to the class. This lesson provides
students with a unique opportunity to specify their own interesting topics or aspects
of a real-world event, determine research methods to solve a problem or improve
understanding, and then present their findings to the class in an innovative manner.

<table>
<tr><td>Glossary Term</td></tr>
<tr><td>online encyclopedias. A collection of encyclopedias on the Internet.</td></tr>
</table>

EXAMPLES

- Use the computer connected to the projector to show the class how to
  navigate the Encyclopedia Websites (CD Supplement 9G).

- Discuss the importance of knowing where the information is coming
  from. Anyone can create a webpage with information on it, but is it the
  truth? How can you find out?

- Prepare lesson guidelines based on grade level and student abilities and
  share them with the students.

- Write the glossary term on the board and discuss the meaning with
  the class.

Check for Understanding

Students should have a good understanding of your expectations for this lesson.
Discuss various concepts and ideas to determine the students' comprehension levels.
If the students do not seem to understand, you may need to teach a section of this
project-based lesson in a different way.

EXAMPLES

- Ask a volunteer to explain how to open and navigate a particular
  Encyclopedia Website (CD Supplement 9G) while another student uses
  the computer connected to the projector to show these steps.

- Ask the students, "How is an actual encyclopedia different from an
  online encyclopedia?" and "How are they the same?"

- Have various students explain the project and the expectations for the
  groups during this lesson.

Guided Practice

This guided activity, assigning groups and topics, will provide the students with a
group and a particular topic. Any procedures required for students as they complete
the project within their assigned groups could be discussed in this section.

EXAMPLES

- Use the Solar System Questions (CD Supplement 9H) to assign topics based on student interest. Share the questions with the class and have them write down on a piece of paper the number of the questions that they are interested in. Then tell the students that if they have No. 1, they should go to a specific place in the room, such as the printer. Continue in this manner until all students are in a group. Be flexible; if some topics generate more interest, allow two groups to work on the same topic.

- Assign groups in a creative manner by hanging large sign-up sheets around the room. Have students share questions or topics they are interested in and write one topic on each sheet. Then have students walk to the sign-up sheet that they would like to research and write their names on the paper. Use this information to assign groups.

- Assign groups and tasks to the group members, and then have each group come up with its own question concerning the solar system. The groups could then think of all that they already know about it and write the facts on a piece of paper.

- Have students think of and share appropriate keywords to type into the search box on the online encyclopedia website that they might use to find information about their particular topic.

Variations for Younger Students

The younger students will probably need to complete the research with more guidance and structure. Give them as much flexibility and room to grow as possible when completing their project(s).

EXAMPLES

- Choose one question or topic to focus on as a class using the Solar Systems Questions (CD Supplement 9H). Have the entire class watch a video or look at pictures concerning the question, and ask students to draw a picture about the topic.

- Display a page from one of the sites listed on Encyclopedia Websites (CD Supplement 9G) on the class screen using the computer projector, and discuss the procedures for navigating and finding information on the site, such as looking for pictures, boldfaced words, and hyperlinks. For younger students, choose only one or two websites.

- Show students an encyclopedia website using your computer, and have students click exactly where you click on their individual computers. Have them sit with their hands folded while you click a few links, and then allow them to click until they arrive at the same page. Continue in this manner so that students learn how to navigate the site.

- Assign projects to the groups with specific guidelines depending upon the age of students in the class.

- Write directions on the board for younger students to follow while working.

Independent Practice

Students will now work in groups using the online encyclopedias to collect and analyze data to solve a problem or to research a topic. The students' ideas will begin to flow as they determine the specific tasks that need to be completed by each group member. Encourage students and show them that you believe in their abilities and ideas as they begin to work interactively and collaboratively. You will be surprised at the innovative thinking that occurs as students work together and immerse themselves in the project.

Establish boundaries and requirements before the students begin to work. This will keep them focused on their project and help them understand all that is expected of them. Remind students about ethical behavior while working online.

EXAMPLES

- Require students to design a timeline for their project completion and keep a log of events with dates, times, and places for specific activities to be completed. Depending upon the type of collaborative activity assigned, you may need to provide more than one class period to complete the project. If necessary, students may also complete some of the work outside of class time.

- Ensure that each student has a specific task and knows what to do. Explain any specific requirements for the research, including an interview, chart, typed information, journals, survey, experiments, or video.

- Help students recognize the various online encyclopedias as credible sources of information as they research. Students could list in a bibliography the specific online encyclopedias that they use.

- Students should learn all they can about the topic using online encyclopedias and make critical decisions to solve the problem. After finding a solution, the students should determine how to present the information to the class in the most effective way.

Assessment

It may be difficult to assess this subjective assignment, so be sure to plan ways to measure student achievement. The assessment method should be made clear to the students at the beginning of the lesson to maximize student potential.

EXAMPLES

- Have students write a postcard to the president of the United States or another politician explaining their opinions about their solar system topic using the Postcard Template (CD Supplement 9I).

- Each student completes a Group Assessment form (CD Supplement 9F) showing the efforts of the other group members. This form could be used as part of their grade for this lesson.

- Evaluate the group presentations based on the clarity with which they explain their answer to the question.

- Make informal observations of collaborative group efforts while the students are working. Record the observations in the grade book.
- During the group presentations, evaluate the students in the audience on their polite behavior and listening skills.
- Instruct students to submit any notes, records, drawings, interviews, and surveys for assessment. Use these to assess the effort put forth by each student.

Closure

Plan a way to conclude the lesson with congratulations and praise for a job well done. Students should feel proud of their group work and achievements. It is important for students to contemplate all of their accomplishments during this project as well as the work of other groups.

EXAMPLES

- Encourage students to discuss any difficulties experienced when working on the project and how these matters were resolved. Also, they could discuss things that they will do differently during the next group project.
- Have students reflect on all they have learned using the online encyclopedias and ways this information could be used to provide solutions to other problems in the real world to increase global awareness.
- Ask the students whether they would rather be part of the problem or part of the solution. This is something that can be applied to many life situations because it is always better to propose a solution than complain and be a part of the problem.
- Encourage students to discuss possible problems that occur at school, such as bullying, locker issues, or safety hazards, and ask them to suggest steps they could take to provide solutions to these situations.

Extension

The thrill of completing a group project using online encyclopedias will probably kindle the interest of many students in the class. Consider other real-world research and activities for accelerated students that will further their abilities and skills.

EXAMPLES

- Encourage students to think of a real-world situation they would like to research individually or with a partner. Work with the students before or after class to determine and monitor their progress.
- Have students type their journal into a website so that each member of the group can view the logs of all group members at any time. This will keep the students up to date with other group members.

- Encourage groups to communicate while working using a telecommunications method such as e-mail, teleconferencing, videoconferencing, or instant messaging.

- Direct students to find a problem in their local community and complete research to come up with a possible solution. Students could then write a letter or contact local politicians to submit their solutions.

- Publish the results of the projects in the school newsletter, on the school website, or in a local newspaper.

- Have students create a bibliography listing the sites used in their groups.

Remediation

Some students may require extra explanation and assistance during this lesson. Each student may need assistance on a different level; try to determine the appropriate individual method of instruction for each student.

EXAMPLES

- Consider the various abilities and leadership skills of the students when grouping them.

- Provide a little extra encouragement to students who may not be intrinsically motivated.

- List on the board or write on paper the steps for completing the individual tasks within the group. This may help students stay focused on the project.

- Provide students with extra time to complete their individual assignments.

Accommodation

Be sensitive to students with special needs or disabilities and make modifications to the lesson depending on individual needs. Consider the best ways to modify the lesson to provide the least restrictive environment for these students.

EXAMPLES

- If possible, assign a student with special needs to a group that will be sensitive and patient with the student.

- Assign a special task within the group, such as listener or observer, to a student with special needs.

- Give alternative assignments and assessments to students with disabilities to ensure achievement. You may want to grade these students on an individual grading scale.

UNIT 10

Web 2.0

Unit Overview

This unit, entitled Web 2.0, includes two lessons: Blogs and Podcasts. In the first lesson, Blogs, students will learn and practice word processing skills while learning about blogs, and then they will create their own blogs. In the second lesson, Podcasts, students will learn about podcasts and incorporate audio and video technology to create their own unique podcasts. At the completion of this unit, students will have a basic understanding of blogs and podcasts as well as increased knowledge of several technology operational concepts.

Unit Goal

To give students an understanding of blogs and podcasts and to teach them to create unique works, a blog and a podcast, using word processing and other technologies.

NETS•S Addressed

1. **Creativity and Innovation**

    Students demonstrate creative thinking, construct knowledge, and develop innovative products and processes using technology. Students:

    - a. apply existing knowledge to generate new ideas, products, or processes
    - b. create original works as a means of personal or group expression
    - c. use models and simulations to explore complex systems and issues
    - d. identify trends and forecast possibilities

6. **Technology Operations and Concepts**

    Students demonstrate a sound understanding of technology concepts, systems, and operations. Students:

    - a. understand and use technology systems
    - b. select and use applications effectively and productively
    - c. troubleshoot systems and applications
    - d. transfer current knowledge to learning of new technologies

Unit Variations for Younger Students

Below are a few ways to make this lesson more suitable for younger students. Several variations have also been noted throughout the unit to assist you further in planning activities for younger students.

EXAMPLES

- Focus on one definition for each lesson. You will probably want to expose students to all of the terms but only require them to learn the meaning of one main term in each lesson.

- Use a central theme, based on something that the students are currently learning, such as nursery rhymes, Thanksgiving, food, families, or the solar system. This will allow students to work with familiar concepts while learning about blogs and podcasts.

- Choose a few older students to assist when younger students begin creating their blogs or podcasts. These mentors not only will be helping the younger students, they also will be strengthening their own technology skills. The older students' self-confidence will be boosted when they act as "teachers."

Room Decorations

Think about ways to change the appearance of the computer lab to increase excitement about blogs and podcasts. The classroom should promote creativity as well as focus the students' attention on the learning concepts. The decorations in the room could be referenced throughout the unit while teaching about blogs and podcasts. The following examples provide decorating suggestions.

EXAMPLES

- Print all or some of the slides from the Blog Slide Show and Podcast Slide Show (CD Supplements 10A and 10I). Staple them to brightly colored construction paper, and display them in the computer lab. You may decide to enlarge and print a few slides using an enlarging machine.

- Designate a bulletin board in the computer lab for the Web 2.0 unit. Use a banner or letter cutouts to title the board "Blogs and Podcasts." Place a border with the unit theme around the bulletin board.

- Select a theme for this unit, such as music, animals, or sports. Decorate the room with creative items based on the theme. Change the desktop background on each computer to a picture of the chosen theme. During the lessons, have students create a blog and podcast based on this theme.

- Create a large pretend blog on the wall or bulletin board based on the favorite sports teams (or another topic) of all students in the school. You could title the bulletin board "Computer Lab Blog." Throughout the unit give students an opportunity to write about their favorite sports team by writing on this board. This is a great way for all students to see that blogs represent real information. The information on this board could be used in the first lesson, entitled Blogs.

Blogs

Objective

Students will learn and practice word processing skills while learning about blogs and then create their own blogs.

Materials and Equipment

- pencil for each student
- dry erase board and markers or chalkboard and chalk
- word processor (Microsoft Word, Writer—OpenOffice.org, Word Pad, or Notepad)
- laser pointer (optional)
- printer (optional)
- computer projection device
- Supplements 10A, 10B, 10C, 10D, 10E, 10F, 10G, and 10H

Supplement List

Below is a list of the lesson supplements that are on the accompanying CD, which is located in the back of this book. Use the CD to open the supplements and modify them, if desired.

SUPPLEMENT	TITLE	FORMAT
10A	Blog Slide Show	PowerPoint Presentation
10B	Blog Facts	Word Document
10C	Word Processing Skills Checklist I	Word Document
10D	Word Processing Skills Checklist II	Word Document
10E	Blog I	Word Document
10F	Blog II	Word Document
10G	Blog I Answers	Word Document
10H	Blog II Answers	Word Document

Procedures

Motivation

Plan an exciting opening activity that will create a sense of anticipation. One of the following motivations could be implemented to focus the students' attention on blogs.

EXAMPLES

- If your school has a blog, or you have a personal blog, you could show the class those blogs on the class screen using the computer connected to the projector.

- Print out a sample blog from a website and read it to the class.

- Remind students about safety on the Internet. It is very important never to give away any personal information about yourself, school, or activities. Have students explain why they should not share personal information on the Internet. Refer to Unit 4, Digital Citizenship, for more information about online safety.

- Ask, "Has anyone ever read a blog?" Have students share these experiences with the class.

- Encourage students to share examples of how blogs are helpful at school or in the community.

- Have students raise their hands if they would like to design their own blogs. Have them share a topic that they could use for their blogs.

- Ask the class "Has anyone ever kept a diary or a journal?" Tell the class that a blog is like a diary or journal, written for everyone to see, on the Internet.

Purpose

Explain that in this lesson you will teach the students about blogs using word processing skills. Provide personal meaning to students by encouraging them to take ownership of the information. If students understand the reason for blogs and the importance of word processing skills, they will be more likely to concentrate on the lesson. Share with the class the importance of being able to type and use a word processor.

Remind students about the importance of being safe when going online. Explain that once you publish something on the Internet it will always be available; therefore, do not write and publish anything on the Internet that you want to keep private.

Instructional Input

In this section, plan an activity that will teach the students about the types and uses of blogs. Consider which method of instruction will best meet the varying ability levels of each class. The following list offers ideas for this discussion.

- Use the computer connected to the projector to show the Blog Slide Show (CD Supplement 10A). As students are viewing the slide show, discuss various facts about blogs and encourage students to participate in the discussion.

- Show a few different sample blogs using the computer connected to the projector. You could choose blogs that may be of interest to the students, such as local community events, political elections, or sports events. You may want to create screenshots of the blogs instead of projecting the actual blog onto the projector because it may be difficult to screen the blog for appropriate material for the classroom since blogs are updated often.

- Hold a class discussion on blogs, explaining their definition and purpose.
    - Explain to the class that a blog is like a journal that is posted online for everyone to read.
    - Show the blog and tell students that blogs are a place to share opinions.

- Choose various students to use the laser pointer to point out different items that they see on the blog website, such as the date, pictures, links, archived files, and posts.

Check for Understanding

Ensure that the students understand the blogging concepts taught in this lesson. Think of a creative way to get all students involved in demonstrating their knowledge of blogs.

EXAMPLES

- Show the Blog Slide Show (CD Supplement 10A) again, and have students give the meanings of the terms before they appear on the screen.

- Have students explain the definition or purpose of a blog.

- Ask the students a few questions about blogs. When students know the answers, they could give a sign such as thumbs up.

Guided Practice

In this guided practice, show students how to use several word processing skills, such as font style, undo, and italics. Think of a fun and innovative way to guide the students while they improve their word processing skills using the information on blogs. Decide which word processor to use with the various classes (Microsoft Word, Writer—OpenOffice.org, Word Pad, or Notepad). You may decide to assign partners so that students are able to share information and help each other during this activity.

EXAMPLES

- Instruct students to open the Blog Facts worksheet (CD Supplement 10B) at their computers and use word processing skills to modify the text on this sheet.

- Have students type some facts on blogs and then modify the text on their sheet. You could have them type some facts that they remember about blogs or copy a few facts from the board. You could also tell them some facts to type onto their computers.

- Using the computer connected to the projector, show students how to modify the text, and allow students to practice at their own computers. You could use a laser pointer to point to the screen to show students exactly where to click on the word processor.

- Choose a student to use the computer connected to the projector to show the class the steps for modifying the text.

- Have students take turns using the laser pointer on the class screen to direct attention to specific places on the word processor, to make sure they know where to click.

Independent Practice

Students will probably be excited to begin using the word processing skills on their own. Explain that students will be working independently at their own computers using word processing skills. You may want to dim the lights to minimize glare on the monitors as students are working. Remind students about the correct keyboarding position. Adjust the activity to enable students to learn based on their abilities.

EXAMPLES

- Have students use the Word Processing Skills Checklist I (CD Supplement 10C) to practice each word processing skill and then place a check in the box next to the skill. Depending on students' abilities in the class, consider assigning only a section of the items on the checklist.

- Have students open the Blog I worksheet (CD Supplement 10E) at their computers and use word processing skills to complete the worksheet. You may decide to print it out and give it to students to complete for homework or when they finish the word processing checklist.

- Show the class how to use several word processing skills, such as change font, insert bullets, or make text bold or italic, using the computer connected to the projector. Have students complete these skills using their computers. It may help to have all students sit with their hands folded, watching until you finish explaining, or students might keep working and miss information that they need.

- Have students use word processing skills to create a blog. The students will not actually upload their blog to the Internet. You could have them upload the blog to a local server. Make up a fun topic or allow students to come up with their own topics and design. Students could pick a topic that they find interesting from the following list, or you could assign one of these topics for the entire class.

- Have students write about a children's book, poem, verse, or other printed material.

- Ask students to write about all that they have learned in the computer lab this year.

- Students create a blog to tell a new student about their school.

- Allow students to gather data using a variety of methods—surveying, collecting online statistics, conducting an opinion poll, or any other method they find interesting. Instruct students to record their data on paper to be used to create the blog.

- Conduct a quick class survey, and then have the class create a blog together based on the data. This will show the students the way to collect data and use this data to create a blog.

- Make up a news report on a local event, the weather, or upcoming events.

- Have students create blogs based on their interests and hobbies, such as baseball, swimming, or art.

- Have students create blogs explaining their favorite subjects, describing why they like these subjects.

Variations for Younger Students

Modify the word processing skills required for each group of students. For younger students, mastering a few of the word processing skills may be more important than knowing how to do every skill on the checklist. Give students an opportunity to learn about word processors at their own levels of understanding.

EXAMPLES

- Instruct students to use the Word Processing Skills Checklist II (CD Supplement 10D) to practice the word processing skill, and then place a check in the box next to the skill. Depending on students' abilities in the class, consider assigning only a section of the items on the checklist.

- Have students open the Blog II worksheet (CD Supplement 10F) at their computers and use word processing skills to complete the worksheet. You may decide to print it out and give it to students to complete for homework or when they finish the word processing checklist.

- Ask younger students to type their names and the name of your school using the word processor. Have students modify this text while learning some basic word processing skills.

- Teach the younger students how to use the "undo" button first. Students will appreciate how easy it is to "undo" their mistakes.

- Have the youngest students type in all caps instead of using the shift keys; it may be easier.

- Show the class how to do one word processing skill at a time using the computer connected to the projector, and then have students repeat this skill using their computers. It may help to have all students sit with their hands folded, watching until you finish explaining, or students will keep working and miss information that they need.

- Take a few minutes and show the class how to do several word processing skills, and then have the students practice the skills and "play" with the word processor at their computers.

- Ask students to choose their favorite color font to use when typing.

- Have the younger students type their names and insert a graphic. Modify their names and the graphic using a few word processing skills.

- Create a pretend class blog. Make up a fun topic such as favorite food, school uniforms, school lunch, holidays, or cell phones allowed at school. Have students share their opinions with the class. Type these opinions on a word processor to create the pretend blog. Students could type one sentence or word into the class blog using the projector, or students could tell you their opinions as you type them. You can get as creative as you like with this activity by including pictures, dates, surveys, and other items typically found on a blog.

Glossary Terms

blog. Short for "Web Log." A website with a personal journal that is usually updated often.

blogger. The person writing the blog.

blogging. Writing a blog.

blogosphere. The collection of all blogs on the Internet.

social networking site. A website where users create personal profiles and communicate with others online. Examples: MySpace, Facebook, Xanga

Web 2.0. A term used to describe the way the World Wide Web is used as social networking where people can easily communicate via online communication including blogs.

Assessment

Students have had the opportunity to learn a lot about blogs and word processing in this lesson. Clearly explain throughout the lesson all that is expected of students. The students' previous knowledge of blogs and word processing skills may be considered when deciding the assessment method.

EXAMPLES

- Collect and check the Word Processing Checklist I and II (CD Supplements 10C and 10D).

- Use the Blog I and II Answers (CD Supplements 10G and 10H) to check students' work. It may be fun to project the worksheet on the screen using the computer connected to the projector and allow students to take turns typing in the correct answers so the class can check their work. This gives students another opportunity to use word processing skills.

- Have students print out the word processing work that they completed about blogs. Remind students to ensure that they typed their names on the top of the page before they print. Collect and assess their work.

- Choose various students to use the computer connected to the projector and show how to do a certain skill on the checklist.

- Call individual students to your computer or go to their computers and ask them to show you how to do a particular word processing skill.

- Observe students as they are working at their computers. Record these observations on a grading sheet. Student participation could also be recorded throughout the lesson.

Closure

Close the lesson by congratulating each student for having learned about blogs and word processing skills. Promote a sense of accomplishment at the completion of the lesson.

EXAMPLES

- Have each student share one new fact about blogs or a word processing skill that they learned today.

- Hang a few of the best word processing papers or worksheets on the Blogs bulletin board.

- For homework, ask students to practice word processing skills and print their work to share it during the next computer class.

Extension

This lesson may have motivated students to want to learn more about blogs and word processors. Think of additional ways to challenge students to expand their knowledge.

EXAMPLES

- Ask students to complete an online tutorial on word processing skills.

- Have students research Web 2.0 and explain how the Internet has recently changed to contain more social networking websites.

- Have students keep a journal for one week that could be a pretend blog.

- Create a blog for the computer lab.

- Instruct students to research the dangers of blogging using personal information and share the information they learned with the class.

- Encourage students to practice different word processing skills that were not discussed in class.

- Have students try different types of word processors and explain what they like about the various types.

Remediation

Throughout the lesson, monitor the students to determine whether anyone is having difficulty in a certain area. If necessary, change the lesson so that students are given many opportunities to succeed. Consider the most effective ways to assist students having difficulty.

EXAMPLES

- Give students who are behind extra time to complete the Word Processing Skills Checklist I or II (CD Supplements 10C or 10D).

- Give students a copy of the Blog Slide Show (CD Supplement 10A) to look at during the lesson or to take home and study.

- Write the word processing skills on the board to show clearly which skills are required during the lesson.

- Ask a student who understands to explain or show how to accomplish the word processing skill to another student who needs assistance. Sometimes it helps to have students explain or demonstrate new skills to other students.

Accommodation

Be sensitive to students with special needs or disabilities and make modifications to the lesson depending on individual needs. Consider the best ways to modify the lesson to provide the least restrictive environment for these students.

EXAMPLES

- Require students with special needs to complete only a section of the Word Processing Skills Checklist I or II (CD Supplements 10C or 10D).

- Have another teacher or aide help students with special needs while they use word processors.

- Provide assistive technology devices to improve the functional capabilities of students with disabilities.

Podcasts

Objective

Students will learn about podcasts and incorporate audio and video technology to create their own unique podcasts or to create a podcast with a partner.

Materials and Equipment

- paper and pencil for each student
- dry erase board and markers or chalkboard and chalk
- iPod or another digital media device (optional)
- microphones, headphones, and video cameras (use to make podcast)
- various children's books, poems, and rhymes (optional)
- computer projection device
- Supplements 10I, 10J, 10K, 10L, and 10M

Supplement List

Below is a list of the lesson supplements that are on the accompanying CD, which is located in the back of this book. Use the CD to open the supplements and modify them, if desired.

SUPPLEMENT	TITLE	FORMAT
10I	Podcast Slide Show	PowerPoint Presentation
10J	Podcast Quiz I	Word Document
10K	Podcast Quiz II	Word Document
10L	Podcast Quiz I Answers	Word Document
10M	Podcast Quiz II Answers	Word Document

Procedures

Motivation

The goal of this activity is to get students excited about podcasts as they imagine all that can be done when creating a podcast. Think about the best way to encourage students in each class to focus on podcasting.

EXAMPLES

- Display an iPod and a few other types of digital media devices on a table in front of the room. Hold up the various devices and talk about their differences and similarities.

- Ask students to raise their hands if they have an iPod or another digital media device.

- Use the computer, an iPod, or another digital media device to download and play an audio or video podcast on an interesting topic that the students will enjoy. If your school has any podcasts or you have a personal podcast, you could allow the class to hear or watch those podcasts.

- Make a video of yourself giving some information about podcasts. Play the video for the students, and then discuss how podcasts sometimes include video.

- Remind students about safety on the Internet. Tell them it is very important never to give away any personal information about themselves, their school, or activities. Have students explain why they should not share personal information on the Internet. Refer to Unit 4, Digital Citizenship, for more information about online safety.

- Ask if anyone has ever listened to or watched a podcast. Ask the student to share that experience with the class.

- Encourage students to share examples of how podcasts are helpful at school or in the community.

- Ask the class if anyone has ever recorded his or her voice or made their own video? Tell the class that a podcast is similar to an audio or video recording that they may have made in the past.

- Hold up a microphone and a video camera. Tell students that they will have the opportunity to create their own podcast during the lesson using recording equipment.

Purpose

Explain that in this lesson you will teach the students about podcasts, and then they will produce a podcast using technology. Encourage students to be creative when planning and designing their own podcast. Students will participate in creating the podcast, allowing them to use technology to be creative.

Remind students about the importance of being safe when going online. Explain that once they publish something on the Internet, it will always be available; therefore, they should not write and publish anything on the Internet that they don't want everyone to know about.

Instructional Input

At this time, plan an activity that will teach the students in the class about the types and uses of podcasts. Consider which method of instruction will best meet the varying ability levels of each class. Encourage students to begin thinking about the type of podcast they would like to create. The following list offers ideas for this discussion.

EXAMPLES

- Use the computer connected to the projector to show the Podcast Slide Show (CD Supplement 10I). As students are viewing the slide show, discuss the various facts about podcasts, and encourage students to participate in the discussion.

- Allow students to hear a few different audio podcasts or view video podcasts using the computer connected to the projector. You could choose podcasts that may be of interest to the students, such as local community events, political elections, or sports events. You should listen to and watch the podcast before showing it to the class because it will be difficult to screen a new podcast for appropriate material.

- Hold a class discussion on podcasting and how it works. You could use some of the following statements about podcasts.

  - Podcasts are different from other files because you can subscribe to podcasts that you want to be downloaded automatically.

  - If you subscribe to a podcast, when new podcasts are posted online the files are automatically downloaded to a specific location on your computer.

  - You can listen to podcasts at any time.

- Have students listen to different podcasts and point out the ones they like, the ones they do not like, and why. This may help students to choose the type of podcast they would like to create. Ask students to think about the topic that they want their podcasts to be about, or you could assign a topic. Students could write down a possible topic and some things they would like to discuss during the podcast.

Check for Understanding

Students should now be familiar with podcasts and how they work. Creatively elicit student responses to determine their understanding of podcasts. Constantly evaluate students and modify the lesson so that students are able to satisfy the lesson's objective.

EXAMPLES

- Show the Podcast Slide Show (CD Supplement 10I) again, and have students give the meanings of the terms before they appear on the screen.

- Have students explain why podcasting is unique.

- Ask the students a few questions about podcasts. If students know the answer they could give a sign such as thumbs up.

Guided Practice

In this section, students will practice using the recording equipment. The maturity level of students in the class will determine the guidance needed from the instructor. Before this lesson, practice using the audio and video software and equipment available to you so that you will know how to use it. Determine your equipment and a plan of action for each class. If your school doesn't have much equipment, maybe you could borrow it from a student, another school, or the local library. *Note:* If students are sharing headsets, you may want to have the students clean the ear pieces with an alcohol swab before they put them on.

EXAMPLES

- Instruct students with easy steps for creating their own recordings. The type of recording equipment available at your school will determine these steps. It may be helpful to write the steps on the board or make a worksheet to pass out to students to use when creating their audio or video files.

- Select students to use the computer connected to the projector to record their names using audio or video. Have another student come to the computer and play the recording. Repeat the steps a few times to ensure that all students understand the process.

- Demonstrate to the class how to use the technology carefully. Have students share why it is important to take good care of the classroom equipment.

Glossary Terms

broadcasting. Distributing audio files via streaming technologies.

iPod. A personal digital media player created by Apple.

podcast. Audio and video files that are downloaded from a website to be played on a computer or a mobile device. The term comes from "iPod" and "Broadcasting."

podcast icon. Podcasts on the Internet are identified by a podcast icon.

podcaster. A person who creates a podcast.

podcasting. The process of making audio or video podcasts available via the World Wide Web.

RSS (Really Simple Syndication) feeds. A file written in XML that can be read on your computer, allowing you to read news or web page snippets within a simple interface.

subscribe. Sign up to automatically receive podcasts when new information is posted.

XML. Extensible Markup Language is a text format used to create RSS feeds.

Independent Practice

Students will now independently create a unique podcast. They will not actually upload their podcasts to the Internet. Determine the best way for each class to create a podcast. Let students know how you are going to grade their work by explaining any criteria you would like them to include in the podcasts. While they are working, encourage students to do their best work and help others sitting next to them if they need assistance. Motivate students to think abstractly and creatively when designing their podcasts.

EXAMPLES

- Have students take the Podcast Quiz I (CD Supplement 10J) to show all that they have learned about podcasts.

- Ask the students to close their eyes and imagine their completed podcast. This will encourage them to plan to create their desired finished products.

- Make up a fun topic or allow students to come up with their own topics and write outlines of their podcasts on paper. Students could pick a topic that they find interesting from the following list, or you could assign one of these topics for the entire class.

  - Have students read a children's book, poem, verse, or other printed material.

  - Ask students to tell about all that they learned in computer lab this year.

  - Have students create a podcast to tell a new student about their school.

  - Allow students to gather data using a variety of methods— surveying, collecting online statistics, conducting an opinion poll, or any other method they find interesting. Instruct students to record their data on paper to be used to create the podcast.

  - Conduct a quick class survey, and then have the class create a podcast together based on the data. This will show the students the way to collect data and use this data to create a podcast.

  - Have students work with partners to locate the data and then use the data to create their own podcast. If students work with a partner, the data could be used to create two different types of podcasts. It will be interesting to see the same data displayed two different ways.

  - Make up a news report on a local event, the weather, or upcoming events.

  - Sing a song. Students could even use musical instruments such as a guitar or violin, if available.

  - Have students create a podcast based on student interests and hobbies, such as baseball, swimming, or art.

  - Ask students to create a podcast explaining their favorite subject and why it is their favorite subject.

Variations for Younger Students

Younger students have a different way of thinking; modify the lesson to meet their needs. The following examples suggest ways to help younger students create a podcast.

EXAMPLES

- Have students take the Podcast Quiz II (CD Supplement 10K) showing what they learned about podcasts.

- Ask younger students to recite a nursery rhyme, such as *Humpty Dumpty*, tell a story such as Pocahontas, or read a book, such as *Cinderella,* for their recording.

- Have the class sing a song such as "Itsy Bitsy Spider," or recite together the alphabet in Spanish and record it. Or you could record each student singing the song individually. This might be a great way to have the class memorize a song, story, or poem because students learn quickly through repetition.

- Instruct all students to create the same recording, such as *Humpty Dumpty*, but allow them to be creative with their voices or do something else creative when recording.

- Have younger students work with a partner to create a podcast.

Assessment

Determine a way to evaluate students authentically, based on their individual accomplishments and creative abilities. Students should have met the lesson's objective by incorporating technology to create a unique podcast.

EXAMPLES

- Use the Podcast Quiz I and II Answers (CD Supplements 10L and 10M) to check students' work.

- Ask students to play their podcasts for the class. As students play their podcasts, check to ensure that they know how to use the software and recording equipment. Grade each student's podcast based on the criteria you told the class when assigning the project.

- Have students submit any outlines or notes they used for their podcasts.

- Check student work individually at their computers. Walk around the classroom and look at the monitors to assess the podcasts when students are finished. The students could also walk around the room in an organized manner to listen to the other students' podcasts.

Closure

Hold a celebration of a job well done, and praise the students who worked hard to create a podcast. Students should have a few moments to contemplate all that they have learned during this lesson.

EXAMPLES

- Encourage students to reflect on the lesson and share some things that they learned about podcasts and creating podcasts.
- Ask students to share interesting facts they learned while using the audio and video recording equipment.
- Present an award to the student who created the most innovative podcast.

Extension

Students may be excited about how easy it is to create podcasts. They may want to create more elaborate podcasts on interesting topics. The following activities may encourage students to go beyond all that was learned in class about podcasts.

EXAMPLES

- Make a podcast to use with your class. Have students subscribe to the podcast to get the newest podcasts automatically.
- Assign students the homework of bringing in an iPod or other digital media device. This would be a great opportunity for students to see different digital media devices.
- Encourage students to use different recording equipment to create their podcasts.
- Upload the podcasts to the school's secure network so that students can listen to other students' podcasts in different classes at the school. Make sure you put the files in a secure place on your school network to protect the students and any personal information they may have discussed on their recordings.
- Show the class how to subscribe to podcasts using RSS feeds or how to use iTunes or another podcast utility.

Remediation

Throughout the lesson observe the students to see if anyone needs extra help or a different explanation. Think about ways to meet the needs of every student most effectively by teaching the lesson again in a different way or by modifying the requirements of the lesson.

EXAMPLES

- Include pictures next to the steps when explaining how to use the recording equipment.

- Ask other students to assist the students who need extra help.

- During independent practice, provide help to the students who need to have the instructions repeated.

- To prompt students to think on their own, ask students having difficulty what they think they should do next. This helps students learn to try something by themselves before asking for help.

Accommodation

Be sensitive to students with special needs or disabilities and make modifications to the lesson depending on individual needs. Consider the best ways to modify the lesson to provide the least restrictive environment for these students.

EXAMPLES

- Do not require students with special needs to write down an outline or notes for their podcast.

- Assist students with disabilities by giving them a short book to read for their podcasts, or just have them say their name.

- Have students with special needs work with partners to create a podcast.

National Educational Technology Standards for Teachers (NETS•T)

All classroom teachers should be prepared to meet the following standards and performance indicators.

1. **Facilitate and Inspire Student Learning and Creativity**

    Teachers use their knowledge of subject matter, teaching and learning, and technology to facilitate experiences that advance student learning, creativity, and innovation in both face-to-face and virtual environments. Teachers:

    a. promote, support, and model creative and innovative thinking and inventiveness

    b. engage students in exploring real-world issues and solving authentic problems using digital tools and resources

    c. promote student reflection using collaborative tools to reveal and clarify students' conceptual understanding and thinking, planning, and creative processes

    d. model collaborative knowledge construction by engaging in learning with students, colleagues, and others in face-to-face and virtual environments

2. **Design and Develop Digital-Age Learning Experiences and Assessments**

    Teachers design, develop, and evaluate authentic learning experiences and assessments incorporating contemporary tools and resources to maximize content learning in context and to develop the knowledge, skills, and attitudes identified in the NETS•S. Teachers:

    a. design or adapt relevant learning experiences that incorporate digital tools and resources to promote student learning and creativity

    b. develop technology-enriched learning environments that enable all students to pursue their individual curiosities and become active participants in setting their own educational goals, managing their own learning, and assessing their own progress

    c. customize and personalize learning activities to address students' diverse learning styles, working strategies, and abilities using digital tools and resources

    d. provide students with multiple and varied formative and summative assessments aligned with content and technology standards and use resulting data to inform learning and teaching

3. **Model Digital-Age Work and Learning**

    Teachers exhibit knowledge, skills, and work processes representative of an innovative professional in a global and digital society. Teachers:

    a. demonstrate fluency in technology systems and the transfer of current knowledge to new technologies and situations

    b. collaborate with students, peers, parents, and community members using digital tools and resources to support student success and innovation

    c. communicate relevant information and ideas effectively to students, parents, and peers using a variety of digital-age media and formats

    d. model and facilitate effective use of current and emerging digital tools to locate, analyze, evaluate, and use information resources to support research and learning

4. **Promote and Model Digital Citizenship and Responsibility**

    Teachers understand local and global societal issues and responsibilities in an evolving digital culture and exhibit legal and ethical behavior in their professional practices. Teachers:

    a. advocate, model, and teach safe, legal, and ethical use of digital information and technology, including respect for copyright, intellectual property, and the appropriate documentation of sources

    b. address the diverse needs of all learners by using learner-centered strategies and providing equitable access to appropriate digital tools and resources

    c. promote and model digital etiquette and responsible social interactions related to the use of technology and information

    d. develop and model cultural understanding and global awareness by engaging with colleagues and students of other cultures using digital-age communication and collaboration tools

5. **Engage in Professional Growth and Leadership**

    Teachers continuously improve their professional practice, model lifelong learning, and exhibit leadership in their school and professional community by promoting and demonstrating the effective use of digital tools and resources. Teachers:

    a. participate in local and global learning communities to explore creative applications of technology to improve student learning

    b. exhibit leadership by demonstrating a vision of technology infusion, participating in shared decision making and community building, and developing the leadership and technology skills of others

    c. evaluate and reflect on current research and professional practice on a regular basis to make effective use of existing and emerging digital tools and resources in support of student learning

    d. contribute to the effectiveness, vitality, and self-renewal of the teaching profession and of their school and community